ALFRED LUNT'S COOKBOOK

THE TESTER'S EDITION

THE FABULOUS LUNTS—
ALFRED LUNT & LYNN FONTANNE.

THE DONNING COMPANY PUBLISHERS
184 BUSINESS PARK DRIVE, SUITE 206
VIRGINIA BEACH, VA 23462

G. BRADLEY MARTIN, PROJECT DIRECTOR
STEVE MULL, GENERAL MANAGER
BARBARA BUCHANAN, OFFICE MANAGER
PAMELA KOCH, EDITOR
SCOTT RULE, GRAPHIC DESIGNER
DEBBIE DOWELL, PROJECT RESEARCH COORDINATOR
SCOTT RULE, DIRECTOR OF MARKETING
TONYA HANNINK, MARKETING COORDINATOR

CATALOGING-IN-PUBLICATION DATA
LUNT, ALFRED.
  THE TESTERS EDITION OF ALFRED LUNT'S COOKBOOK : THE NEVER-
BEFORE-PUBLISHED, MUCH-SOUGHT-AFTER RECIPE COLLECTION OF
BROADWAY'S GREATEST ACTOR, ALFRED LUNT.
    P. CM.
  INCLUDES BIBLIOGRAPHICAL REFERENCES AND INDEX.
  ISBN 978-1-57864-417-9 (HARD COVER : ALK. PAPER)
  I. COOKERY. I. TITLE.
  TX714.L875 2007
  641.5--DC22
                                          2007002759

PRINTED IN THE UNITED STATES OF AMERICA AT WALSWORTH PUBLISHING COMPANY

MOST PHOTOS BY WARREN O'BRIEN
FROM THE O'BRIEN FAMILY COLLECTION
AT WHS © TCF OR FROM THE
TEN CHIMNEYS COLLECTION

TeN CHIMNeYS

PRESENTS

THE TESTER'S EDITION OF

ALFRED LUNT'S

COOKBOOK

THE NEVER-BEFORE-PUBLISHED, MUCH-SOUGHT-AFTER, RECIPE COLLECTION
OF BROADWAY'S GREATEST ACTOR, ALFRED LUNT

THE TESTER'S EDITION OF

ALFRED LUNT'S

COOKBOOK

"MR. LUNT NOT ONLY INVENTS, HE ACQUIRES BY WHATEVER MEANS

NECESSARY THE RECIPES HE COVETS."

COLLIER'S, 1933

Broadway's greatest actor was also one of its greatest chefs.
The recipes contained in this first-printing were complied by Alfred Lunt
during his glorious retirement to his Wisconsin retreat, TEN CHIMNEYS.

The original set of Alfred's typed pages is presented here, virtually unedited
(and largely untested), for your pleasure and review. Readers and chefs are encouraged to
send reactions to Ten Chimneys Foundation for consideration in subsequent printings.

Tester's Edition Results

PLEASE SEND YOUR RESULTS, EDITS, AND EXPERIENCES,

ALONG WITH THE RECIPE TITLE(S) AND PAGE NUMBER(S) AND

YOUR NAME AND CONTACT INFORMATION TO:

TEN CHIMNEYS FOUNDATION
ALFRED'S COOKBOOK
POST OFFICE BOX 225
GENESEE DEPOT, WI 53127

ALFREDSCOOKBOOK@TENCHIMNEYS.ORG

THANK YOU

TABLE OF

CONTENTS

THE TESTER'S EDITION OF
ALFRED LUNT'S
COOKBOOK

Alfred Lunt and wife Lynn Fontanne are widely considered the greatest acting team in the history of theatre. Not willing to simply coast on their extraordinary natural talent, the Lunts were consummate professionals. Their passion for excellence and commitment to the art of live theatre, and the ART OF LIVING, was legendary. Graciously entertaining dear friends at their Wisconsin home, TEN CHIMNEYS, was a joy for the Lunts. Alfred would spend all afternoon in the kitchen, pop upstairs to dress for dinner, and then reappear to escort the group into the dining room for the perfect meal. Lynn and Alfred's dazzling guests—Noël Coward, Helen Hayes, Laurence Olivier, Katharine Hepburn, Alexander Woollcott—were themselves dazzled.

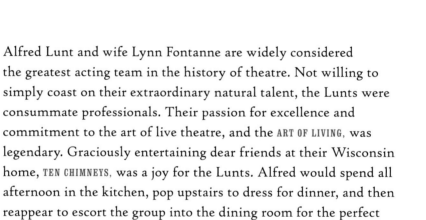

"EVERY TIME I WAS VISITING WITH THE LUNTS IN GENESEE DEPOT I WAS IN A SORT OF DAZE OF WONDER...THE DINING ROOM, THE TABLE, THE CHINA, THE SILVER, THE FOOD, THE EXTRAORDINARY CARE AND BEAUTY AND TASTE...A SORT OF DREAM, A VISION."

KATHARINE HEPBURN

In 1958, the Lunts began the American run of what would be their final stage performance—THE VISIT. The play opened in the newly dedicated Lunt-Fontanne Theatre on Broadway, honoring the couple for their extraordinary contribution to American theatre. On hiatus during rehearsals of THE VISIT in Europe, Lynn and Alfred found themselves on a much-needed break, but without the opportunity to return home to Ten Chimneys. Since "vacation" had always meant time for new creation and growth, a substitute was required. So, Alfred, at age 65, completed a course of study at Le Cordon Bleu. He passed, as Lynn quipped, with "flying saucepans." His Diplome de cuisine Bourgeoise et de Patisserie was the culmination of his lifelong passion for cooking.

Once the Lunts retired from the stage in 1960, they lived in their beloved Ten Chimneys year-round—and spent many happy years there enjoying the extraordinary retreat they had created together. Alfred passed away in 1977, at the age of 84. Lynn passed away six years later, in 1983, at the age of 95. A monument at their grave reads, "Alfred Lunt and Lynn Fontanne were universally regarded as the greatest acting team in the history of the English speaking theatre. They were married for 55 years and were inseparable both on and off the stage."

Alfred's own typed cookbook pages were left behind, concealed in a closet in Ten Chimneys' Main House Library.

ALFRED LUNT

ALFRED LUNT IN HIS 1907 CARROLL COLLEGE SMASH HIT, "PRIVATE SECRETARY." NOT LONG AFTER THIS SHOW, ALFRED WOULD TAKE OFF FOR BROADWAY.

"One of America's foremost stage actors, Alfred Lunt made his debut with a Boston stock company in 1912. He first set foot on a Broadway stage in 1917, and two years later scored his first significant success as the title character in CLARENCE. In 1922, he married British actress Lynn Fontanne, and for the next 35 years the team of Lunt and Fontanne reigned supreme along the Great White Way. Their string of stage successes included AMPHYTRION 38, IDIOTS' DELIGHT, and THE VISIT, not to mention their sublime collaborations with actor/playwright Noël Coward (PRIVATE LIVES, DESIGN FOR LIVING). By nature and inclination a stage actor, Lunt made only a handful of film appearances, most of them during the silent era; one of his least characteristic film roles was in D.W. Griffith's SALLY OF THE SAWDUST, in which he played third fiddle to Carol Dempster and W.C. Fields. Outside of a guest appearance in 1943's STAGE DOOR CANTEEN, Lunt and Fontanne appeared together onscreen only once, in a 1931 adaptation of their stage success THE GUARDSMAN, for which they both received Academy Award nominations. After his retirement, Alfred Lunt lived the life of a gentleman farmer in Genesee Depot, WI, occasionally phoning a Milwaukee radio talk show to offer gratis gardening tips to other listeners."

HAL ERICKSON on ALFRED LUNT

TAKEN FROM THE ALL MOVIE GUIDE, *THE NEW YORK TIMES*

IN HIS OWN WORDS

"I'M SUPPOSED TO BE WRITING A COOKBOOK. I WANT TO TELL YOU!
WHAT CAN I DO?! IT'S THE SAME THING OVER AND OVER:
PUT IT IN THE OVEN. TAKE IT OUT. HOW MANY WORDS ARE THERE?
IT MUST BE THE SAME. STIR AND SPOON. AND AFTER A WHILE, YOU LOOK
AT THE GODDAM THING—FOR IT IS NO GREAT LITERARY EFFORT,
YOU KNOW—IT IS SO BORING YET, IT MUST BE CLEAR.

AND I ASKED TRUMAN CAPOTE. I SAID, 'WILL YOU TELL ME HOW, WHEN
YOU MAKE A PIE CRUST, JUST DESCRIBE THIS? I WANT IT IN WORDS. HOW
WOULD YOU "DO THIS, NOW DO THAT" IN A FEW WORDS?' I ASKED.
'I COULD SHOW YOU HOW, BUT PUT IT IN WORDS...' AND HE COULDN'T."

AN INTERVIEW WITH ALFRED LUNT FROM "ACTORS TALK ABOUT ACTING"
BY LEWIS FUNKE & JOHN BOOTH, 1961

"THE MAJORITY OF RECIPES IN THIS BOOK WOULD NOT COME UNDER THE
HEADING OF 'HAUTE CUISINE' BUT THEY ARE TASTY, ECONOMICAL FOR
THE MOST PART, SIMPLE TO MAKE, AND THOUGH FAMILIAR TO SOME MAY
NOT BE TO OTHERS—AND SO ARE HUMBLY SUBMITTED TO THOSE WHO
LIKE TO COOK, TO THOSE WHO HAVE NEVER COOKED BUT WISH TO, AND
TO THOSE WHO DO NOT WANT TO COOK BUT HAVE TO."

ALFRED LUNT

IN HIS OWN WORDS

Alfred's notes on . . .

HERBS, EXTRACTS AND SAUCES
USED IN RECIPES

HERBS	EXTRACTS	SAUCES
Rosemary	Vanilla	Kitchen bouquet
Thyme	Almond	Tabasco
Sweet basil	Lemon	Worcestershire sauce
Marjoram		
Cardamom seed		
Dill		
Tarragon		
Sage		

WHOLE AND GROUND SPICES
USED IN RECIPES

WHOLE SPICES	GROUND SPICES	"FOUR SPICES"
Black pepper	Black pepper	2 tsp. ground black or white pepper
Cloves	White pepper	
Celery seed	*(White pepper is*	2 tsp. ground nutmeg
Mustard seed	*sharp and invisible)*	1/2 tsp. ground allspice
Coriander seed	Cloves	1/4 tsp. ground cloves
Allspice	Cinnamon	*Mix and keep in a small*
Nutmeg	Allspice	*tightly covered jar, to be*
Caraway seed	Nutmeg	*used in white sauce, fish*
Stick cinnamon	Cayenne	*balls, etc.*
Bay leaves	Mace	
Gumbo filet	Paprika (sweet)	
	Curry powder	
	Ginger	
	Turmeric	

MEASUREMENTS

There is pleasure in reducing "shortening" from cups to weight. You know how messy it is to measure out 1/2 of a cup of butter, pushing it down, scraping it out, discovering the cup you want or flour is smeared with fat, etc. So a postal scale will eliminate this awkwardness, measuring in *weight* from a tablespoon on up.

SCALE

2 cups butter	1 lb.	1 tbsp. butter	1 scant oz.
1 cup butter	1/2 lb.	2/3 cup butter	5 oz.
1/2 cup butter	1/4 lb. (4 oz.)	1/3 cup butter	2 1/2 oz.

BUTTER

Many of the recipes in this book call for butter. You may substitute of course, which is your own business, but if you do, the taste of many of them will be considerably altered, as in some of the cakes—even in broiled fish. Half oleomargarine and half butter, thoroughly mixed is sometimes unidentifiable, and half beef dripping and half butter for potato frying is delicious. Your pocketbook and imagination will be your best guides.

KITCHEN ACCESSORIES

There are a few KITCHEN GADGETS particularly recommended: those sets of metal or plastic cups, 1 cup, 1/2 cup, 1/3 cup and 1/4 cup; ten-cent egg separator; a set of measuring spoons, 1 tbsp., 1 tsp., 1/2 tsp., 1/4 tsp.; wooden spoons, long handled flat bowled type; and perhaps above all an electric knife sharpener. Most women cooks seem to have a passion for dull knives, trying to sharpen them on the edge of a crock or the rim of the stove. If you can't procure or afford an electric sharpener, at least learn to use a steel and sharpen your knives constantly.

The quickest and most accurate way to use a KNIFE for slicing is with a sawing movement. Don't press the knife straight down, but shove foreward with a long stroke. Don't bother to cut while pulling the blade back. And learn to

KITCHEN ACCESSORIES CONTINUED

chop with a knife. Use a straight edged blade at least 8 inches long. Hold the tip of blade with the left hand thumb and index finger firmly down on the board and keep it there. Lift the knife up and down, with the handle held in right hand. It has more freedom of movement than at first imagined, as the knife can be swung by the right hand forward and back making almost a complete arc. Previous to chopping, thinly slice the meat or vegetables and make a pile of them in center of board.

The use of NEWSPAPERS on table or counter is highly recommended. They act as a sort of silent tweeny and are tremendous timesavers. Spread them out in two or more sheets, as they do at a wrapping counter, and as you work roll up your debris and put the package at once in the garbage pail or incinerator.

And wear an APRON—not one of those dainty little things, but a great big white one with long strings crossed at the back and tied in the front, through which to draw an old towel which is not for effect but for use. It may quickly become soiled, this towel, and that's exactly what it's for.

"A SHARP KNIFE IN THE KITCHEN IS WHAT WIT IS TO NOËL COWARD."

ALFRED LUNT

KITCHEN ETIQUETTE

May I suggest that if you are fortunate enough to have a cook and yet wish to astound your family by passing a few culinary miracles yourself, first *warn* the cook of your intention, appoint a mutually convenient time, then proceed to gather together all your utensils and food stuffs, set them on spread-out newspapers in a secluded place in the kitchen, and not until then begin your labors. *And*—when finished wash up, sweep up, leaving the room cleaner than you found it.

BREAKFAST

People who aren't themselves until ten, shouldn't get up until ten. But a pleasing breakfast might help.

There are many superb cooks who, for some unaccountable reason, serve the most appalling breakfasts: lukewarm coffee, tepid tea, burnt toast, eggs boiled, with small white tumors shoving through their cracks or fried like cork pads. It is an important meal and can be a happy one.

In your own house surely you should get what you want. It's no more trouble, really. For instance, toast browned evenly on both sides and while hot spread with soft butter to the edge! If for some reason the toast burns, for heaven's sake scrape it off into the sink.

DECORATIONS

A "Grand Rapids" old-fashioned leaf type of lettuce is most satisfactory. It has a large, flat, fan-shaped leaf with ruffled edges and is of a beautiful green color. It will twist or tear into many shapes.

Parsley tied in tight bunches (cut stems off close) in many sizes will keep for days.

Slice off a little piece of the bottom of a fully ripe tomato so it will stand up firmly. Make an incision at stem end and stick in a bunch of parsley. Do the same with a lemon or half a lemon.

Very firm aspic chopped into tiny cubes – for cold meats.

Lemon slices cut 1/8 inch thick. Cut a line from center and through rind. Twist the points in opposite directions – like a dancer doing a split in the "can-can." This can also be done with cucumbers.

The last two decorations are useful for canapés.

IN HIS OWN WORDS

WINE

Using cheap wines in cooking is like attending the opera in an undershirt. Use only the best grades and this also applies to extracts, particularly vanilla, which your druggist should be able to procure for you.

TIMING

Just one more thing: unless experienced, it is a little difficult to cook and have ready at a specified time an entire meal. A list made out beforehand of what you are to serve and the order in which each should start cooking to be completed in time is a help. And an early preparation of meat and vegetables is no hindrance either. Say for instance you are having roast duck, peas, new potatoes and a dessert. Make the dessert in the morning and put it in the ice box. Prepare your duck for roasting and put it in its pan. Later scrub the potatoes, put them in their pot, and lastly shell the peas (they shouldn't be washed), and put them in theirs. Two or three hours before dinner, put the duck in the oven. Fifty minutes before dinner put on a kettle of water. Forty minutes before dinner start boiling potatoes, and twenty minutes before dinner start cooking the peas. Use double boilers for keeping things hot (or improvised ones: small pan in a larger one of steaming water. These home steam pans will keep hot even off the stove, if not left too long. Good for ten minutes at least.)

"I AM DELIRIOUSLY HAPPY . . . JELLY MAKING—RASPBERRY JELLY, CURRANT, CHERRY, BLACKBERRY . . . AND FENCE MAKING AND TREE TRIMMING AND SCRUBBING AND PAINTING . . . THE GARDENS, IN LATE AUGUST, ARE FAIRLY BURSTING WITH FLOWERS AND VEGETABLES."

ALFRED LUNT AT TEN CHIMNEYS, 1933

MEN IN THE KITCHEN

TAKEN FROM "HE LIKES TO COOK," *BETTER HOMES & GARDENS*, AUGUST 1962

If you are indifferent to the taste, textures, and looks of food, if your time is limited to minutes, if you pale at the very thought of washing dishes—don't cook.

Stick to instant coffee, frozen dinners, and a brick of ice cream. Let your wife (or with luck, your maid) clean up, and you'll be much better off, as will the rest of your family. Better still, draw out your savings and go to a restaurant.

If, on the other hand, you're tired of "store-bought victuals" and have an urge to whip up a real homemade meal, the following cooking prompts may save you time, money, hysteria—possibly a divorce.

Suppose you want to put on a Sunday brunch or dinner, plan ahead a day at least. Take a pad and pencil and sit alone in your car in the garage to write down everything you intend to serve and in what order. And see to it that all the ingredients are in the house the night before, so you won't have to wake your wife to ask where she keeps the mustard, or isn't there any? It's even a good idea to set out the pots and pans. That will save a lot of crawling around and banging through those lower cupboards the next morning.

Seventy-five years ago, ALFRED LUNT and LYNN FONTANNE, the most revered acting team in American theatre history, conjured a haven called TEN CHIMNEYS. Created with the same humanizing wit and passion for perfection that distinguished their stage performances, Ten Chimneys is the Lunts' most enduring and tangible legacy. For decades, their idyllic retreat beguiled and inspired the country's finest actors, writers, designers, directors, and artists.

Ten Chimneys Foundation

In 1996, Ten Chimneys came perilously close to destruction through commercial development until Joseph W. Garton—the late Madison-area restaurateur, theatre historian, and arts advocate—led a public opposition to this unthinkable fate. Dr. Garton spent the next two years connecting with community and civic leaders and national experts in various fields. In November of 1997, twenty-four prominent civic leaders came together to form the Board of Trustees of Ten Chimneys Foundation. In January of 1998, Ten Chimneys Foundation took legal ownership of the estate and began emergency repairs. The Foundation then began extensive research and planning for restoration, preservation, and program development—continuing to collaborate with dozens of experts and advisors. In 1999, the United States Postal Service issued a commemorative Lunt-Fontanne postage stamp. Ten Chimneys was one of the first historic sites to be named an official project of Save America's Treasures, a public-private partnership between the White House Millennium Council and the National Trust for Historic Preservation. Hundreds of dedicated volunteers, generous donors, and other Foundation leaders made extraordinary strides leading up to May 26th, 2003—when Ten Chimneys opened to the public for the first time (on what would have been the Lunts' 81st wedding anniversary).

TEN CHIMNEYS, the National Historic Landmark estate created by Alfred Lunt and Lynn Fontanne, is open to the public as a world-class house museum and national resource for theatre, arts, and arts education.

The MISSION of the Foundation is to preserve and share the buildings, furnishings, collections, and grounds of a national treasure—Ten Chimneys, the estate created by Alfred Lunt and Lynn Fontanne; to serve as a continuing resource and powerful inspiration for theatre, the arts, and the art of living; and to offer public programs consistent with the Lunts' varied interests and core values while maintaining the integrity and intimacy of this extraordinary estate.

Our VISION for the future of Ten Chimneys is to be nationally recognized as the most memorable and inspirational historic house tour in the country; "the place" for aspiring and practicing theatre professionals to gather; a source of inspiration for the art of living; and an accessible and active member of the local and arts communities.

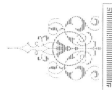
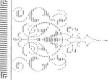

ACKNOWLEDGEMENTS

We are honored to finally bring ALFRED LUNT'S recipes to the table. Ten Chimneys Foundation wishes to thank all of the stalwart VOLUNTEERS who made this printing possible. In particular, our heartfelt, full-belly thanks are extended to:

LUCILLE JUSTIN Ten Chimneys Foundation's first volunteer, the late beloved Lucille Justin, for her original transcription from Alfred's original manuscripts;

VERNA SCHMIDT for her tireless, thoughtful, and well-organized pursuit of articles, quotes, and any-and-all-Alfred-cookbook-miscellany;

CHRISTINE GESICK for the extensive formatting, categorizing, sorting, and good-old-fashioned typing she provided to ensure the integrity of Alfred's collection;

Ten Chimneys FRIENDS AND ENTHUSIASTS who clamored for Alfred's recipes. *Enjoy.*

This cookbook was lovingly edited by ERIKA KENT, Vice President of Ten Chimneys Foundation. Final text was fastidiously reviewed by Foundation staff member, AMANDA SHILLING. Most photos by WARREN O'BRIEN from the O'BRIEN FAMILY COLLECTION. The publishing process was shepherded by SEAN MALONE, President of Ten Chimneys Foundation, with assistance from staff member JACK BRADWAY. Design was provided by ERIC HARMS and SCOTT RULE. Acknowledgements also go to participants of our Oral Histories Project and Ten Chimneys Foundation Curator, CAIT DALLAS.

This first printing is dedicated to the much-missed friend
who truly ensured the Lunts' legacy:

DR. JOSEPH GARTON
(1946-2003)

"HE MADE GOOD SAUCES."

HORS D'OEUVRES

Alfred and Lynn in the Cottage Kitchen of Ten Chimneys.

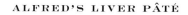

ALFRED'S LIVER PÂTÉ

1 pound calves' liver	1/2 tsp. white pepper
1/4 pound lean veal	1/8 tsp. ginger
1/2 pound port fat, unsalted	salt
1 onion, large	anchovy paste
1 cup cream, a generous cup	3 eggs, beaten
4 Tbsp. flour	brandy

Wash and wipe meat, cut in three pieces and grind with onion three times. Add cream and flour, spices and salt, 3 squirts of anchovy paste, each 3 inches long, and put through Waring Mixer until a very fine texture is reached. Pour into bowl over beaten eggs and beat vigorously. Then pour into a bread pan. Tie a double piece of wax paper over top. Set in a large pan of water (a water bath) and bake in a 250° oven for 1½ hours. Unmold when cold. Wash the tin, rinse with cold water and pour in aspic [amount of aspic not mentioned in manuscript] to the depth of 1/2 inch. Set in icebox to harden. Trim off all sides of pâté 1/4 of an inch and replace carefully on aspic in tin. Pour over this aspic to fill in sides and top and re-set in icebox. When firm, unmold and slice. The bottom aspic may be decorated with eggs, beets, onion greens, etc., before pâté is re-set. The pâté crusts can be used for family sandwiches.

ALFRED'S PORK SAUSAGE

2 pounds pork, 1/3 fat	1½ tsp. pepper, freshly ground
1/4 pound bread, cubed and soaked in	1 tsp. sugar
1/2 cup water	1/2 tsp. rosemary, sieved
1 Tbsp. salt	1¼ tsp. nutmeg
	1/4 tsp. sage

[No instructions on preparation in manuscript]

SOUPS

Helen Hayes, Alfred Lunt, and Lynn Fontanne dining in the Garden Terrace Room of the Main House of Ten Chimneys.

ALFRED LUNT'S
COOKBOOK
TESTER'S EDITION

ALFRED'S OLD TIME BEET SOUP (CLEAR)

2–3 pounds beef soup meat

1 knuckle of veal, if possible,
    all meat and bone cut
    into pieces

1 tsp. salt

beef fat, for searing

3 large onions, sliced

3 large carrots, sliced

1 bunch celery tops

4 beets, peeled and sliced

parsley, small bunch

1 extra onion, carrot, leek

6 whole peppercorns

2 cups beets, grated or
    chopped

2 Tbsp. tomato juice

NOTE: THE INGREDIENT "TOMATO JUICE" DOES NOT APPEAR IN THE INSTRUCTIONS BELOW.

Sear the meat until brown. Then the sliced onions and carrots. Cover well with cold water, bring to a boil and add celery tops, the 4 sliced beets, the parsley, the extra onion, carrots, the peppercorns. Cover and simmer 3–4 hours. Strain. Cool overnight and then remove all fat. Replace on stove, add the grated beets and bring to a boil. Remove from heat at once as boiling causes the soup to turn brown. Strain through cheesecloth. Correct seasoning. Serve hot or cold—with helpings of sour cream and piroshki.

ALFRED'S BOMBAY BISQUE

4 Tbsp. butter

1/3 cup onion, finely chopped

1/3 cup celery, finely chopped

1/3 cup carrot, finely chopped

1/2 cup apple, chopped

1 tsp. curry

1 quart chicken broth

1 Tbsp. juice from chutney

cream to taste, or 1/2 cup

Mix together onion, celery, carrot, and apple and sauté in butter until golden. Stir in curry and add this to hot chicken broth. Cook slowly until vegetables are tender. Put through Waring Mixer, then re-heat, adding chutney juice and cream. Serve cold or hot, but it's better cold. If any fat rises to top when cold, skim it off before serving.

22

"LUNT ACQUIRED HIS UNCANNY SKILL BACK IN THE DAYS WHEN, ON FIVE
DOLLARS A WEEK, HE WAS ENDEAVORING TO KEEP BODY AND SOUL TOGETHER
... THE ONLY WAY THAT COULD BE ACCOMPLISHED WAS BY COOKING HIS
OWN MEALS OVER A STUDENT LAMP IN A THIRD FLOOR BACK."

COLLIER'S, "THE CHEF'S ROLE," 1933

ALFRED'S CLEAR BORSCHT (SERVES 4)

NOTE: THE INGREDIENTS "PINCH OF SUGAR" AND "LARGE ONION" DO NOT APPEAR IN THE INSTRUCTIONS BELOW.

pinch of sugar

3 cans water

1 carrot

3 celery stalks, with leaves
small bunch parsley

1 small tomato, or 3 Tbsp.
    tomato juice

3 medium-sized raw beets,
    peeled and sliced

5 peppercorns

1 very full cup raw beets,
    about 3 grated

1 large onion

Put consommé, water, carrot, celery, parsley, tomato, sliced beets, and peppercorns into kettle and simmer for 1½ hours. Strain through fine sieve. Replace liquid in kettle and add grated beets, bring to a boil, no longer as boiling will turn color brown, and strain again. Add salt if necessary. Serve hot or cold with sour cream and piroshki. Canned beets may be substituted, and if so, add 1/2 cup of their juice.

ALFRED'S COURT BOUILLON

2 quarts water

1/2 cup each, chopped onion,
    carrot, and celery

1 clove

1/2 bay leaf

8 peppercorns

small bunch parsley, and dill,
    if procurable

2 tsp. salt

2 Tbsp. vinegar

3 Tbsp. lemon juice

Boil the above all together until water is well flavored—about 15 to 20 minutes.

ALFRED'S KEYCLUB TOMATO SOUP (SERVES 3–4)

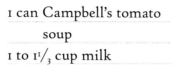

1 can Campbell's tomato
soup
1 to 1¹/₃ cup milk

1 large dill pickle, kosher
type with garlic and
dill

Add milk to 1 can of soup and in it slice the dill pickle. Let stand 3 hours or more. Heat, remove pickle and serve. You can "top" with whipped sweet or sour cream.

ALFRED'S ONION SOUP

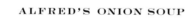

1 can onion soup
1/2 can water

3 Tbsp. port wine

Heat soup and water. When hot add the port wine. Serve with French bread croutons and grated Parmesan cheese. Or French bread croutons spread and toasted with Parmesan cheese.

ALFRED'S SOUP STOCK

2 pounds brisket, chuck or
    shoulder
1 soup bone, cracked
1/2 Tbsp. salt
2¹/₂ quarts water
6 peppercorns
4 carrots

1 parsnip
3 leeks, with parts of leaves
3 onions, medium
bunch of parsley
6 allspice
1 clove

Rinse meat in cold water and cut into 3- or 4-inch cubes. Place in kettle with bone, add cold water, and bring to a boil. Skim, add vegetables and spices and bring to a boil and skim again. Cover and let simmer for three hours. Strain, cool, and when fat solidifies on top, remove it. If you wish to clarify it, return to kettle and add 2 egg whites and shells. Bring slowly to boil stirring constantly. Boil 3 minutes. Let stand 25 minutes, and then strain through fine cheesecloth.

ALFRED'S VICHYSSOISE (POTATO SOUP - HOT OR COLD)

1 cup potatoes, diced
2/3 cup onions, finely sliced
1/2 cup leek, finely sliced,
    white part
2 cups water

1 tsp. lemon juice
1¹/₂ cups chicken broth
1/2 cup cream
1 Tbsp. chopped chives
salt and pepper, to taste

Boil potatoes, onions, and leeks in 2 cups of water to which lemon juice has been added, with pot covered, until the potatoes are very soft. Let cool slightly and pour into electric mixer and blend until a smooth texture. Return to pan. Add chicken broth, heat thoroughly and then add the cream. Sprinkle with chopped chives. If this is to be served cold, be sure it's really cold and serve in cups that have been chilled in the refrigerator.

ALFRED'S POTATO SOUP

3 potatoes	1/2 tsp. salt
3 leeks or onions	2 cups water
2 or 3 Tbsp. celery (chopped)	1 cup milk

Cut potatoes, onions, and celery, add salt and put on stove and cook 1/2 hour until soft. Sieve. Add 1 cup of milk (or 2) and boil up. Thicken with cornstarch, or butter and flour method. Instead of water, use 2 cups of chicken broth.

TAKEN FROM *UNITED NATIONS RECIPES FOR WAR RATIONED COOKING*, P. 15

ALFRED'S CLAM CHOWDER

2 to 3 cans (or frozen) condensed clam chowder	whole allspice

Prepare canned or frozen clam chowder according to the label instructions, except add 4 to 6 whole allspice when heating. The allspice will float, and as they look like a mistake, skim them off before your chowder goes to the table. Make a lot—two or three cans worth—as people like it. Serve with toast or pilot biscuit. You'll find you're quite pleased with yourself and your guests with you.

TAKEN FROM "HE LIKES TO COOK," *BETTER HOMES & GARDENS*, AUGUST 1962

SALADS

THE LUNTS AND FRIENDS ON THE GROUNDS OF TEN CHIMNEYS
IN GENESEE DEPOT, WISCONSIN.

ALFRED'S COLD EGGS WITH SHRIMP AND MAYONNAISE

4 hard-boiled eggs
1 pound shrimp, cooked and
　　shelled
1/2 cup mayonnaise

1/3 cup cream
pinch of salt
curry, to taste

Cut eggs in two and place in center of dish already arranged with lettuce. Surround eggs with shrimps. Put mayonnaise (mixed with cream) over eggs and serve. It is better to marinate shrimp first in a little French dressing, but not necessary. Or add curry powder (first mixed with water) to mayonnaise if you like.

ALFRED'S DEEP DISH TOMATO SALAD (SERVES 6)

5 large tomatoes, fully ripe
salt and pepper
1/4 cup sugar
1/4 cup chives, chopped

1/4 cup dill, chopped
1/4 cup onion, chopped
1/4 cup parsley, chopped
vinegar

Peel, remove green core and slice tomatoes. Arrange a layer of slices on bottom of deep glass bowl, and over this sprinkle salt, sugar, freshly ground pepper, chives, dill, onion and parsley; then another layer of tomatoes and seasoning until dish is full, ending up with seasoning. If no fresh dill is available, substitute a dill pickle chopped very fine. Pour over a few tablespoons of vinegar. Press the whole mess down gently with the hands (or a saucer) so that the juice will rise to top. Taste and add more vinegar if you wish. Set in icebox for at least one hour, and serve. Proportions are difficult to suggest.

ALFRED'S TOMATO ASPIC (SERVES 4)

When fresh tomatoes are scarce, try at least for
once a simple tomato aspic without spicing it up.

2 cups tomato juice, or   sugar
       strained canned   1 Tbsp. gelatin
       tomatoes   1/4 cup water
salt and pepper

Heat juice, and season only with salt and pepper to taste and 1/2 teaspoon sugar. Add
gelatin dissolved in water. Simmer a few minutes until dissolved in juice. Pour into a
mold that has been rinsed in cold water. Chill until firm. Remove onto serving plate.
Decorate with lettuce and parsley or both. If a ring mold is used, fill with: shrimp
mayonnaise, cucumber in sour cream, cottage cheese with a separate bowl of thin
mayonnaise, or a cooked vegetable salad.

BREAKFAST &
BRUNCH

ALFRED AND LYNN DINING POOLSIDE AT TEN CHIMNEYS.

ALFRED LUNT'S
COOKBOOK
TESTER'S EDITION

ALFRED'S ROYAL CHEESE DISH (SERVES 6)

4 cups bread (about 5 slices, 1" thick, not stale), cut into 1" slices, buttered thinly, then cubed
1/2 pound good sharp cheddar cheese, cut into 1/2" cubes

3 eggs, beaten
2 cups milk
salt and pepper
butter

Place cubes of bread in well-buttered, 6-cup casserole dish (8" diameter, 3" deep). Add squares of cheese and mix. Beat eggs, add milk, salt and pepper to taste and pour over mixture in casserole. Let stand at least an hour or longer. Stick triangles of buttered bread 1/2" thick (about 8) around top edge of crown. Bake in 350° oven for about 50 minutes or until, if pierced by a knife, it comes out clean. When leaving oven it should be lightly browned and puffed up.

ALFRED'S BAKED OMELET
(THE USES OF THIS OMELET ARE MANIFOLD.)

3 eggs, beaten
1 cup milk, scalded and cooled

salt and pepper
1 Tbsp. butter

NOTE: THE INGREDIENT "1 TBSP. BUTTER" DOES NOT APPEAR IN INSTRUCTIONS BELOW.

Beat eggs and milk, salt and pepper to taste, and pour into shallow casserole (or baking dish) and bake in 375° oven (15 to 20 minutes) until egg has set. Or you can use individual casseroles (shallow), in which case baking requires less time. Can be served plain from dish or removed and split and filled, or can be filled when lower egg level and sides are set and then replaced in oven to complete baking, or filled when completely baked. It can be used as a dessert, split and filled with hot apricot preserves or any other desired hot fruit. It can be turned out on platter (bottom side up), seared with a red-hot fork, sprinkled with sugar, then liquor, which is lighted on being served. It can be covered or filled with: creamed vegetables; creamed lobster or shrimps; creamed spinach; creamed or sautéed mushrooms; creamed fish; creamed Swedish fish balls, or fish balls and lobster sauce; tomatoes, with onions, cooked down to a thick spread; cubed ham (fried); onions, sliced and sautéed; freshened salt herring, with pieces overlapping in diagonal rows. Or after beating eggs and milk, stir in sautéed mushrooms and bake in small buttered glass bread pan (serve from dish). Or with mixed vegetables, peas, cubed carrots, turnips, etc.

ALFRED'S CHEESE DELIGHT (SERVES 1)

4 ounces cream cheese

2 Tbsp. milk

salt and pepper

1 tsp. chopped onion or
chives

1 slice bread, toasted on
one side

1/2 cup cheddar cheese,
shredded

paprika

Beat cream cheese and milk, salt and pepper to taste, and stir in the onions or chives. Toast the bread on one side only and lay it, toasted side down, on baking dish and spread with mixture. Cover this with the shredded cheese. Sprinkle with paprika and broil until puffed and brown.

ALFRED'S CHRISTMAS OMELET

NOTE: THE INGREDIENT "2 TBSP. CREAM" DOES NOT APPEAR IN INSTRUCTIONS BELOW.

6 eggs

2 Tbsp. cream

salt

sugar

1 Tbsp. rum

a very little grating of
    lemon or orange rind

2 Tbsp. butter, for frying

1 cup or more of heated
    mincemeat

1/4 cup rum, with which
    to flame finished
    omelet

Beat eggs until well blended. Then beat in salt, sugar, rum, and gratings of orange or lemon rind. Make into omelet. Spread mincemeat onto it. Fold and slide onto platter. Pour over heated rum, set it alight, and serve.

ALFRED'S COTTAGE CHEESE BALLS
(TO SERVE WITH FISH, VEAL, ETC.)

1/4 pound dry cottage cheese

1 egg, separated

1/2 cup freshly grated white
    breadcrumbs, no crust
    used

1/2 tsp. salt

dash cayenne and white
    pepper

1/4 cup breadcrumbs,
    brown

2–3 Tbsp. butter

NOTE: THE INGREDIENTS "BREADCRUMBS, BROWN" AND "BUTTER" DO NOT APPEAR IN INSTRUCTIONS BELOW.

Put the cheese through a sieve and mix together with the egg yolk, the white breadcrumbs, salt, pepper, and cayenne. Then stir in the egg white, whipped up but not dry. Let stand, in the refrigerator, for an hour or two. Form into balls, the size of walnuts. Drop carefully into gently-salted, boiling water and cook for five minutes. Remove to paper napkin but keep them warm. To make fresh breadcrumbs: Rub day old bread through a sieve (go round and round inside) or grate it, or put in blender.

ALFRED'S DESSERT (SWEET) OMELET

(Basic recipe)   2 Tbsp. sugar
6 eggs   pinch of salt

Separate two of the eggs. Beat whites stiff. Add sugar to the four eggs and the two yolks and beat lightly. Add salt. Fold in whites. Fry as for usual omelet. Add a few gratings of lemon and/or orange peel. Fill with apricot jam or mincemeat (see Christmas Omelet, page 36). Or, when it is placed on serving dish, pour warm, dark rum over and around, and ignite.

ALFRED'S DESSERT OMELET

4 eggs, separated   1/2 cup apricot jam, pureed
6 tsp. sugar   1/4 Grand Marnier
pinch of salt   other fillings and liquors
2 tsp. butter   listed below

Beat egg yolks, 6 teaspoons of sugar and salt until thick and light in color. Fold carefully into stiffly beaten egg whites. Melt butter in frying pan (twist, turn pan about so some of it will cover the sides as well as the bottom) and when it begins to bubble, pour in egg mixture. Cook over low heat—it burns quickly. Remove from fire when nearly set—the middle should be moist—and place under broiler just until the top is firm. Slide half onto platter and on the side pour on filling and fold over. Sprinkle with sugar—score with red-hot fork. Pour over 1/4 cup of liquor and ignite, or better still, pour liquor into jam, ignite and pour over omelet. With 2/3 cup mincemeat, use 1/3 cup brandy. With strawberry jam, use 1/3 cup Cointreau. With currant jelly, use Grand Marnier. With cherry or peach jam, use Kirsch. Or use whatever combination you fancy.

ALFRED'S EGGS À LA TRIPE

3 Tbsp. butter	1¹/₂ cups hot milk
1/2 pound ordinary onions,	4 hard-boiled eggs
thinly sliced	Parmesan and Romano
2 Tbsp. flour	grated cheese
salt and pepper	

Melt butter, and add onions—cover. Simmer until soft. Don't let them color. Turn off fire. Add flour, salt, pepper. Pour on the milk, stir, and let simmer a few minutes. Sauce should be thick and creamy. Put sliced (in strips) egg whites on bottom of buttered gratin. Scatter yolks that have been put through sieve over top. Put sauce over. Sprinkle with grated cheese. Brown in hot oven.

ALFRED'S EGGS AND LIVER PASTE IN ASPIC RING (SERVES 4)

4 hard-boiled eggs	4 cups aspic
1/3 cup liver paste	

Shell the eggs and carefully cut in two lengthwise without cutting or breaking the yolks. Fill each cavity of the egg whites with liver paste or foie gras (not liver sausage), and press together in the form of a whole egg. Set these and the yolks aside in a cool place. Pour some aspic into a 6-cup ring mold and let harden. Then alternately place on this a "whole" egg, then an egg yolk, etc. Fill the mold with cool but not firm aspic and set in icebox to harden. Unmold and serve with a thin mayonnaise. If foie gras is used, thin down with cream.

ALFRED'S EGGS MADRID
(THIS IS A LUNCHEON OR LATE SUPPER DISH.)

scrambled eggs

creamed chicken

tomato sauce

chopped parsley

Make a ring of scrambled eggs on a round serving dish, fill with creamed chicken and surround eggs with tomato sauce. Sprinkle with finely chopped parsley. Serve hot.

ALFRED'S HARD-BOILED EGGS

Put eggs in pan and cover with cold water. Let come to a boil and simmer 20 minutes. Then plunge eggs into cold water and let them remain in it until they are cold. In this matter the shells can be removed easily and the eggs will be really hard boiled.

ALFRED'S PLAIN OMELET

2 eggs	salt and pepper
1 tsp. water	1 Tbsp. butter

Beat eggs, water, and a little salt and pepper lightly with a fork. There must be no foam. Heat pan until a drop of water will sizzle on it, or test with wetted finger as you would a flat iron. Add butter and let melt, rolling pan about so that butter will coat all sides. Pour in eggs and cook shaking them now and then until bottom is firm. Tip pan and let uncooked egg rush to side, pushing cooked omelet back. When all is firm but moist on top, tip pan again and fold over omelet in half. Slide onto serving dish.

ALFRED'S SCRAMBLED EGGS

1 Tbsp. butter	salt and pepper
1/2 cup milk or cream	4 eggs, slightly beaten

Use a double boiler, chafing dish or any ordinary saucepan. Heat butter, add milk. Salt and pepper, to taste. Then stir in slightly beaten eggs and stir, scraping sides, until cooked to taste. Finely cut chives, chopped parsley, or sliced mushrooms may be added while cooking.

"EGGS—THERE ARE ALWAYS EGGS IN EVERY ICE-BOX. WHAT TO DO WITH AN EGG? MR. LUNT HAS HAD MANY INSPIRATIONS. IF THERE'S A LITTLE KETCHUP HANDY, JUST DOUSE IT ON SCRAMBLED EGGS AND MIX IN. OR TAKE SOME CAVIAR AND MIX INTO THE SCRAMBLED EGGS. THIS GIVES THAT CERTAIN SOMETHING—VERY FASCINATING."

COLLIER'S, "THE CHEF'S ROLE," 1933

ALFRED'S SOUFFLÉS

Soufflés are not difficult if you have an accurate oven and can resist opening the door for 40 minutes after you set in the casserole. Be sure the oven is preheated to 350°.

CHEESE SOUFFLÉ

2 Tbsp. butter	1/4 tsp. salt
3 Tbsp. flour	1/4 tsp. pepper
2 cups milk, heated	4 eggs, separated
1 cup sharp cheese, grated or shredded	

Melt butter in top of double boiler, stir in flour, and then the hot milk. Stir until thick and smooth. Add cheese. Let it melt and stir until smooth. Add salt and pepper. Remove from stove and let cool. Stir in egg yolks, one at a time, and beat until smooth. Pour this very slowly over the egg whites whipped stiff, constantly mixing lightly and completely, keeping it always foamy. There must be no white or yellow streaks left at the end of this process. Pour into a well-buttered, 7-inch casserole, and bake in a 350° oven for 50 to 55 minutes.

"RELAXING FOR THE SUMMER AT THEIR HOME IN WISCONSIN'S LAKE COUNTRY, LUNT STILL COMES UP WITH SOME CURTAIN-RAISERS IN THE KITCHEN, WHERE HANGS HIS DIPLOMA FROM THE CORDON BLEU OF PARIS."

"HE LIKES TO COOK,"
BETTER HOMES & GARDENS, 1962

Alfred's Tips:

TO FRY EGGS

Have a generous amount of fat (butter, bacon or ham) ready and hot in frying pan, into which break the eggs—though unless expert, it is safer to break them in a saucer first (not more than two at a time) and slide them in. Salt and pepper and baste them with hot fat from side of pan, which will put a thin white glaze over top, or turn with a perforated pancake turner, or just fry them sunny side up—as you like. Eggs fried in hot olive oil will make the whites resemble lace doilies, if you want the whites to look like lace doilies.

FISH & SEAFOOD

THE LUNTS ON THEIR HONEYMOON.

ALFRED LUNT'S
COOKBOOK
TESTER'S EDITION

To one quart of water, add 1 teaspoon salt. Bring to a boil and immerse fish. One-half cup milk added to water will help whiten fish, such as halibut, cod, haddock, etc.

ALFRED'S CANNED SALMON MOUSSE

1 pound tin salmon, drained, skinned, and boned	1 packet plain gelatin, dissolved in 1/2 cup water
juice of 1/2 lemon	fresh dill, minced, to taste
3 heaping Tbsp. mayonnaise	
3 heaping Tbsp. heavy cream	

Put all ingredients in blender. Mix well, pour into serving dish, refrigerate at least four hours. It is better made the day before. This recipe, doubled, feeds six.

ALFRED'S FISH BALLS (BOILED) (SERVES 4–6)

1 pound fresh or frozen
    haddock or cod
2 tbsp. butter (2 ounces)
1 egg
1/2 cup milk

1/4 cup potato flour
3/4 tsp. salt
1/8 tsp. white pepper
1/8 tsp. "Four Spices"

It is inadvisable to use this recipe unless you have an electric beater. Put fish through meat grinder (use finest blade) one or two times. Add butter and beat 15 minutes. Then beat in the egg, then the milk, and finally the flour. Add salt, pepper, and "Four Spices" and beat for 15 minutes more. The easiest way to make balls of this mess is to drop a smallish teaspoonful into the palm of your hand and shape it around with the spoon. Drop into a kettle of simmering salted water (1 teaspoon to quart) and cook until done, about 8 to 10 minutes. Serve in a cream sauce, which can be flavored with a pinch of curry. Good in a ring of noodles or mashed potatoes, sprinkled with chopped parsley.

ALFRED'S EASY LATE SUPPER OF FISKEBOLLER (NORWEGIAN FISH BALLS)

Alfred's White or Cream
    Sauce, Light recipe
1 pinch curry

1 can Norwegian (or Swedish)
    fish balls, drained
uncooked rice
chopped parsley

A late supper can be prepared before you start out for your evening's entertainment—with the assistance of a pair of double-boilers. For instance, in the top of one, make a medium white sauce (see Alfred's White or Cream Sauce, Light for Vegetables and Fish, page 164)—stir with a wire whisk and you'll have no lumps. Now add a pinch of curry—just enough to give a faint flavor—dump in a drained can of Norwegian fish balls. There you have Fiskeboller! (Or Fiskbullar, if you buy Swedish fish balls.) Set it over the hot-water section, turn heat very low, and it will keep appetizing and very hot. Use the other pot for rice. When serving, sprinkle the Fiskeboller with chopped parsley. This with a salad tossed behind the scenes, and a dessert of cheese with fruit compote is simple and good.

TAKEN FROM "HE LIKES TO COOK," *BETTER HOMES & GARDENS*, AUGUST 1962

"HE [ALFRED] LOVED TO COOK. HE COULD SPEND ALL DAY COOKING FISH."

J. HALE (ARTIST APPRENTICE AT TEN CHIMNEYS),
FROM TEN CHIMNEYS FOUNDATION'S ORAL HISTORIES PROJECT

51

ALFRED'S LOBSTER SALAD IN CUCUMBERS

The flavor of cucumber slightly permeates the salad and makes the dish doubly attractive. Slice large (12-inch) cucumbers in two and scrape out seeds. Chill in icebox. Then fill generously with lobster salad and set on lettuce leaves. They must obviously be served on "individual plates." Shrimp or mixed cooked vegetable salad may be substituted.

ALFRED'S SALMON IN ASPIC SQUARES

2 cups fish stock or
   consommé
1½ Tbsp. gelatin
1/3 cup cold water
1 small can salmon or 1 cup
   fresh boiled salmon

1 Tbsp. lemon juice
salt and pepper, to taste
1/2 cup mayonnaise, heavy
olives

Heat fish stock or consommé and add gelatin, which has been dissolved by pouring it on the cold water. Remove from fire and let cool but not solidify. Pour some of this into a square or oblong shallow pan to the depth of 1/2 inch. Place in icebox. In the meantime, mash and mix thoroughly the salmon, lemon juice, salt and pepper and a teaspoon of mayonnaise and spread this over aspic in pan when it has become firm. Then over this spread a thin layer of stiff mayonnaise. Then with a knife mark it off in squares and in the center of each square place a slice of olive. Return to icebox, and when very cold, carefully pour over more aspic to the thickness of 1/2 inch. (If aspic in kettle has become hard or lumpy, warm it a little.) In using last gelatin "cover" use a large spoon, pouring it on slowly from one corner and then tipping pan so it will cover without disturbing the mayonnaise and olives. Again return to icebox, and when solid, cut the squares, lifting them out carefully with a spatula onto a serving dish.

"I REMEMBER HAVING MY FRENCH RELATIVES HERE AND HE DECORATED A SALMON FOR US, WITH ALL THE GELATIN AND ALL THE SORTS OF LITTLE BITS OF THIS AND THAT, AND IT WAS KIND OF A SHOWPIECE, REALLY. HE LOVED TO DISPLAY WHAT HE KNEW ABOUT COOKING, AND I THINK HE PROBABLY KNEW QUITE A BIT."

W. ESCHWEILER (WIFE OF A TEN CHIMNEYS ARCHITECT),
FROM TEN CHIMNEYS FOUNDATION'S ORAL HISTORIES PROJECT

ALFRED'S SHRIMP (TO BOIL 2 1/2 POUNDS)

Peel raw shrimps and remove black thread at back. Place in pot adding 1 stalk celery cut in large pieces, 1 medium onion cut in half, 1/2 green pepper, teaspoon salt and 6 whole peppercorns, stalk of dill if available or 1 bay leaf. Add cold water so it will cover shrimps by 2 inches. Bring to a boil and let simmer 1/2 hour. Remove shrimps and save liquid strained for future use.

ALFRED'S SHRIMPS ARNAUD (SERVES 4)

1½ pounds shrimp, shell before boiling; there will be about 9½ ounces after cooking	1/4 tsp. sugar
	1/4 tsp. coarse ground pepper
	1 tsp. dry mustard
	several dashes of Tabasco sauce
1 tsp. salt	

Add:

1/2 clove garlic, chopped	2½ Tbsp. bottled horseradish
4 Tbsp. olive oil	2 tsp. chopped chives
2 Tbsp. vinegar	2 tsp. chopped watercress, if available
1 Tbsp. chopped onion	

Mix well, pour over shrimps. Let stand 2 hours, stirring occasionally, and serve on lettuce leaves.

TO BROIL FISH
(QUANTITIES ARE DIFFICULT TO SPECIFY)

fish	salt and pepper
butter	lemon
fine breadcrumbs	

Choose a shallow pan, round or rectangular, in which the slices of fish will fit snugly. Smear the bottom of pan with a small quantity of butter and then place in it the fish, skin side down. Sprinkle with salt and pepper and then fine breadcrumbs. Dot generously with butter. Preheat oven to 400°. Place fish close under broiler (if electric, but not a full flame if gas) and begin basting as soon as butter has melted and runs to sides of pan. Watch fish closely and baste frequently until done, but not dry. It should be juicy, soft, and rather puffy. Remove to hot platter and pour over it some browned melted butter in which you have squeezed a little lemon juice. Decorate with twists of lemon slices. If bluefish, salmon, whitefish, trout, herring, mackerel, or any fat fish, do not use breadcrumbs—or extra browned butter.

TO FRY FISH

Freshwater fish such as bass, pike, croppies, sunfish, perch, catfish, bullheads, etc., are best cleaned, skinned, and filleted, but brook trout and saltwater fish such as porgies, butterfish, pompano, smelts, flounder, etc., need only be cleaned. Sprinkle fish with salt and pepper. Dredge lightly with flour. Let stand awhile if possible. Put butter or half butter and half margarine in preheated pan. (Bacon grease tends to make fish taste too much like bacon. Even on fishing trips, a can or two of butter, instead of lard or bacon fat, is suggested. When cooking outdoors, fish need not be floured.) When fish is brown on one side, turn and brown on other. The quicker cooked the better, but be careful not to burn.

MAIN DISHES

MEAT

ALFRED AND LYNN IN THE GARDENS OF TEN CHIMNEYS

ALFRED LUNT'S
COOKBOOK
TESTER'S EDITION

ALFRED'S BAKED WHOLE CALF'S LIVER

1 calf liver, a whole one or half	peppercorns
1 cup dried breadcrumbs, coarse	1 onion, sliced
1/4 pound bacon	1 cup sour cream, or flour and
1/4 cup onions, chopped	sweet cream
salt and pepper	1 pound bacon, fried and
butter	crushed
allspice	

Carefully cut tough veins and tubes from liver. Lay it out as flat as possible and spread with a stuffing made of breadcrumbs, fried bacon, cut in tiny pieces, the chopped onion, and salt and pepper to taste. Fold meat over as to conceal stuffing completely and tie with string in the manner of a loined roast. In an iron pot, melt butter, and in it brown the liver on all sides. Then add 3 cups broth (consommé water) [consommé not mentioned in ingredients], the allspice, peppercorns and sliced onion. Cover tightly and either cook slowly on top of stove or in oven for 3 hours, turning meat every half hour or so. When done, remove meat, keep hot and add sour cream to liquid. Let come to boil, then strain. Thicken as for Alfred's Pan Gravy recipe (see page 162). Remove strings from meat. Place on platter and cover with bacon, which has been fried crisp and then crushed. Replace in oven to keep warm. Then serve with the sauce in a separate dish. Omit stuffing is you choose. In this case, lard liver with strips of salt pork. This is a rich but tasty dish.

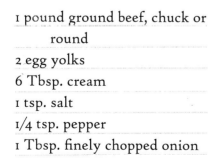

ALFRED'S BEEF À LA LINSTRÖM (SERVES 4)

1 pound ground beef, chuck or	1 Tbsp. finely chopped capers
round	3 Tbsp. finely diced pickled
2 egg yolks	beets
6 Tbsp. cream	6 Tbsp. finely diced boiled
1 tsp. salt	potatoes, medium-sized
1/4 tsp. pepper	3 Tbsp. butter, for frying
1 Tbsp. finely chopped onion	

Grind beef (without fat) very fine. Add egg yolks and cream gradually and stir vigorously. Season with salt and pepper, then mix in, with a fork, the chopped onion, capers, beets, and finally the potatoes. Form into cakes 1" thick and brown quickly in hot melted butter. Place in hot dish, pour over remaining melted butter and serve immediately, with sautéed or French fried potatoes.

ALFRED'S BEEF GOULASH (SERVES 4–6)

1½ pounds onion

1 clove garlic, optional

1 Tbsp. or more mild paprika

1 tsp. tomato paste

2 pounds beef, round or
    rump

1/2 tsp. caraway seeds,
    optional

4–5 potatoes

Preheat stewing pot, and in it melt 2 tablespoons of fat, lard, or vegetable fat. Fry the sliced onions and garlic until golden. Add the paprika and stir it in. Then the tomato paste, then the beef cut in 2- or 3-inch cubes. Stir around until the meat is well seared. Cover the meat with boiling water. Tie the caraway seeds in a little bag and put that in. Let simmer, covered, until meat is very tender, about 2½ hours. Remove the bag of caraway seeds. Add the potatoes, peeled and cut in halves or quarters, and cook covered until done. If, while simmering, the water evaporates too much, add more water to make up for it.

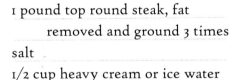

ALFRED'S BEEF PATTIES WITH CAPER SAUCE

1 pound top round steak, fat
    removed and ground 3 times

salt

1/2 cup heavy cream or ice water

1/8 pound butter

freshly ground pepper

2 Tbsp. chopped capers

2 Tbsp. hot water

This is very simple and if made quickly and deftly it can be delicious. The whole process should not take more than five minutes. Beat up lightly the ground beef, salt, and cream or ice water. Form into plump patties (4–6) and fry quickly in the hot butter, turning only once. Do not overcook, as they must be pink inside. Grind over this some pepper. Remove to serving dish and keep warm. Add capers to remaining butter in pan. Stir them about, add the 2 tablespoons of water, stir again, and pour over patties. Serve at once. Grilled tomatoes and sautéed potatoes are a good accompaniment.

ALFRED'S BEEF POT ROAST

4 or more Tbsp. fat *

3½ to 5 pounds beef, round or rump

1 Tbsp. salt

1/2 tsp. sugar

3 cups brown stock, or 1 can consommé and 1 can water

10 peppercorns

1 bay leaf

1 or 2 large onions, peeled and sliced

(All pot roasts, stews, and goulashes are better the day after cooking.)

Sauce:

1 Tbsp. butter   2 Tbsp. flour

Melt fat in iron kettle (with a tightly fitting cover) and in it brown the meat (this is important) on all sides, top, bottom first, then sides by holding with fork or sticking a fork into each side and resting them on pot rim. When seared, remove meat and pour off all the grease. Replace meat, sprinkle with 1 tablespoon salt and the sugar, and add hot stock, peppercorns, bay leaf, and onions and cook slowly for 4 to 5 hours. Keep tightly covered and turn meat now and then. When done, pour off liquid and make a sauce. There should be at least 2½ cups of liquid. Serve with potato pancakes, potato dumplings, boiled, browned or mashed potatoes.

*DON'T USE BACON OR HAM GREASE, BUT CUT SOME FAT OFF

ROAST OR HAVE THE BUTCHER GIVE YOU SOME AND "TRY IT OUT"

IN KETTLE, OR USE LARD OR VEGETABLE FAT.

"DINNERS WOULD BE ROASTS, FRESH VEGETABLES, RICE,

POTATOES, SOMETIMES A SALAD AND THEN, OF COURSE,

ONE OF THE DESSERTS SHE [LYNN] LIKED."

M. ROLAND (WORKED FOR THE LUNTS),

FROM TEN CHIMNEYS FOUNDATION'S ORAL HISTORIES PROJECT

ALFRED'S BOILED FRESH TONGUE

2 medium onions	6 parsley sprigs
1 large carrot	10 peppercorns
3–4 celery stalks and leaves	

Cover tongue with boiling water and add above ingredients. Cook covered 3 hours or until tender.

ALFRED'S CORNED BEEF HASH
(THIS IS VERY LIGHT AND PALATABLE.)

5 medium potatoes	1 pound corned beef,
1/2 tsp. salt	canned or fresh
1/2 tsp. ground black pepper	3 Tbsp. butter
1 large onion	

Boil potatoes in their jackets, not too well done or they will be mushy. Chill and then peel. Chop them in a wooden bowl and sprinkle with the salt and pepper. Remove to a separate dish. Then chop the onion very fine and set aside. Finally, chop the beef. To this add the potatoes and onion and toss lightly with a fork. Have an iron frying pan piping hot, and put in the butter. When melted, add the hash. Do not press down but add a few bits of butter to the top and sprinkle over with about 1/4 cup hot water. Cover and cook slowly, now and then stirring it up and about with the fork, for about 20 minutes.

ALFRED'S ROAST BEEF HASH

Made the same as Corned Beef Hash (see page 61), only use 2 large onions instead of one.

ALFRED'S CROQUETTES

1 cup ground meat	pepper, to taste
1/2 tsp. grated onion	parsley
1 tsp. finely chopped green pepper, if desired	

[A good way to use up cold meats (except pork). Pot roast is particularly tasty.]

Make a heavy white sauce of:

4 Tbsp. flour (1/4 cup)	1/8 tsp. white pepper
4 Tbsp. butter	1 cup hot milk
1/4 tsp. salt	

Stir together with a wooden spoon flour, butter, salt, and pepper in top of double boiler, and add, gradually, hot milk. Stir until well cooked. It should be very thick. Then add ground meat mixture, stirring in well. Spread this 1" thick on a plate and put in refrigerator to harden for at least 1 hour. Remove and shape into croquettes 2" or 2¹/₂" long and 1" thick. Roll first in saucer of flour (or breadcrumbs), then in a shallow dish of well-beaten eggs, then in a plate of crumbs. Place in refrigerator for 1 hour. Fry in deep fat until golden brown and serve with a sauce. Good also, instead of piroshki, with beet soup. In this case, make small ones.

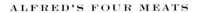

ALFRED'S FOUR MEATS

1 smoked tongue

2 pounds Canadian bacon

3 pounds rolled veal roast

3 pounds beef tenderloin

consommé

Madeira

butter

corn starch or potato flour

salt and pepper

NOTE: THE INGREDIENT "CONSOMMÉ" DOES NOT APPEAR IN INSTRUCTIONS BELOW.

The amount of meat depends on the number of people you wish to serve. This recipe serves 8 generously. All the meat can be cooked a day or two before serving except the beef tenderloin. It is an exceptionally showy dish and not as much work as it looks in print. Boil the tongue and the Canadian bacon, and leave them in water (they were cooked in) until needed. Pot roast veal, making sauce, adding 1/4 cup Madeira and substituting corn starch for flour. Keep until needed. Two hours before dinner, heat tongue, bacon, and veal, wrapped separately in aluminum foil and heated in oven or in a covered kettle with a little water at the bottom. Cook tenderloin. Thinly slice the meats and place them diagonally in rows on hot platter in this order: beef, bacon, veal, tongue. Glaze with a little of the sauce and serve. The dish should be elegantly decorated. Serve the sauce separately. There is no waste as meat not used can be served on other days. No beef will be left over.

ALFRED'S FRIED CALF'S LIVER

If some of the liver is too full of tubes and veins, cut them out carefully with a pair of manicure scissors. Soak slices of calves' liver in milk or skim milk (to cover) for at least one hour. Then drain meat and dry on paper towels or cloth. Sprinkle lightly with salt and pepper on both sides and fry quickly in hot butter, turning constantly. The meat should be pink inside when ready to serve—not overdone. The process takes only 2 to 3 minutes. The best way is to first heat a frying pan to a point where it sizzles if touched with your fingertip. Then add butter or butter and margarine mixed.

Gravy:

1 tablespoon of cream may be added to fat in pan, and a pinch of nutmeg. Pour over meat.

ALFRED'S MINCEMEAT
(MAKES ABOUT 6 QUARTS)

5 pounds boiled lean beef and liquid in which it was cooked	2 quarts molasses
	2 quarts sweet cider
	1 Tbsp. mace
6 pounds sliced apples, weigh after peeling and coring	1 Tbsp. cloves
	1 Tbsp. pepper
	1 Tbsp. allspice
1 pound suet, chopped fine	3 Tbsp. cinnamon
3 pounds raisins	2 Tbsp. salt
2 pounds currants	1 quart brandy
1 pound dark brown sugar	1 pint Madeira

Cook the beef in as little water as possible and when well done, chop fine in a bowl. Do not grind. Put in large pot and add liquid in which beef was cooked. Chop (do not grind) apples and suet, add to meat and then add all the other ingredients except brandy and Madeira. Stir thoroughly. Put over a low flame and simmer slowly until cooked through. This does not take long once it's heated through. Remove from stove and when cool, add brandy and Madeira. Put in jars and seal. Keeps for years in a cool place—if you can resist that long. Add more brandy if you think advisable.

3 lbs. beef, no fat, chuck

Cook slowly, 2–3 hours, in a little water to prevent burning, or in a pressure cooker for 1/2 hour in as little salted water as possible. Chop fine, using a chopping bowl or board—do not grind.

5 pounds tart apples, peeled, cored, and chopped	1/2 pint boiled cider (2 cups cider reduced by quick boiling to 1 cup)
1/2 pound chopped suet	1½ tsp. salt
1½ pounds raisins	1½ tsp. pepper
1 pound currants	1½ tsp. mace
1/2 pound brown sugar	1½ tsp. allspice
1 pint molasses	1 Tbsp. cinnamon
1 quart cider	1 Tbsp. ground nutmeg
	1½ tsp. cloves

Mix thoroughly and heat slowly until heated through. Cool slightly and stir in 1 pint brandy and 1 pint Madeira. Pack in sterilized jars and cover tightly. Will keep for months in cool place. More brandy and Madeira may be added just before serving.

ALFRED'S MIXED GRILL (SERVES 4)

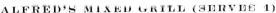

4 lamb chops	4 large or 12 small mushrooms
4 lamb kidneys	4 small tomatoes
8 slices bacon	salt and pepper, to taste
4 sausages	

Broil meats, mushrooms, and tomatoes quickly, and after arranging on hot platter, add hot juices from broiling pan. Serve with French fried potatoes and a green salad. Broil chops and sausages and tomatoes in separate pans. Fry bacon, remove, and keep warm, and in bacon grease fry kidneys. Mushrooms can be sautéed. This is a job, but good.

ALFRED'S ROAST LEG OF LAMB WITH COFFEE (SERVES 6–8)

4–5 pounds leg of lamb	1 large onion, sliced
1 tsp. salt	1 cup coffee, with 2 lumps
pepper	sugar and cream
2 cups water, or stock	

Gravy:

1 Tbsp. butter	1 tsp. pepper
1 Tbsp. flour	

Rub meat with salt and pepper and dust lightly with flour. Brown in hot oven, 450°; then reduce heat to 350°. Add water or stock and sliced onion; cover and roast covered for 3 to 4 hours, basting occasionally. If water dries out, replace it. One hour before done, pour over the coffee and continue roasting and basting. When done, remove to platter and make gravy. The addition of the coffee with cream and sugar added, which can be set aside at breakfast time, is truly good. It's an old Swedish trick and makes as fine a lamb sauce as you've ever curled a lip over.

ALFRED'S ROAST PORK WITH MUSTARD (SERVES 4)

3$\frac{1}{2}$ to 4 pounds rib roast, loin	pepper
1$\frac{1}{2}$ tsp. dry mustard	2 cups water
1 tsp. salt	

Have the butcher split the ribs at base. Fill this crevice with the dry mustard. Sprinkle with salt and pepper and light dusting of flour. Place in pan and brown in hot (450°) oven. Then add 2 cups water, cover, reduce heat to 350°, and roast, basting occasionally, for 3$\frac{1}{2}$ to 4 hours.

ALFRED'S SAVOURY POT ROAST

3$\frac{1}{2}$ to 5 pounds round or rump	10 peppercorns
4 Tbsp. fat	1 tsp. salt
3 cups brown stock, or 1 can	3 Tbsp. vinegar
consommé and 1 can	2 Tbsp. brandy, if desired
water	2 Tbsp. sugar or syrup
10 whole allspice	a few short ribbons of anchovy
1 or 2 onions, sliced	paste
1 bay leaf	

Sauce:

1 Tbsp. butter	2 Tbsp. flour

Prepare and cook as in preceding recipe (see Alfred's Beef Pot Roast, page 60) except that after browning meat you sprinkle top of it with vinegar, brandy, and sugar (or syrup) and smear on anchovy paste. Then continue as for Alfred's Beef Pot Roast. This recipe is not as elaborate as it sounds, and the result is a very tasty one indeed—and a poorer grade of meat can be used in this manner.

ALFRED'S MEATLOAF (SERVES 4)

1 pound lean ground chuck

1/3 cup rice

1 cup boiling salted water

1/2 cup chopped onion

1 Tbsp. butter

1 cup coarsely grated
    zucchini

2/3 cup sour cream

1/4 cup chicken stock

salt and freshly ground
    pepper

paprika

minced parsley

Line bottom and sides of a pie plate with the meat; salt and pepper it, and set aside while you prepare the filling. Preheat the oven to 375°. Heat 1 cup water to boiling, add salt, and cook the rice in it 20 minutes. Drain the rice and place in a bowl. Sauté the onion in the butter till limp and add to the rice. Stir in the zucchini and sour cream, and season lightly with salt and pepper. Pour into the meat shell, pour the stock over the pie—loosening its sides to let the stock run down around the meat—and carefully place in the oven. Bake 40 to 45 minutes, or until the meat is done and the center is puffed and starting to turn straw-colored. To serve, sprinkle with paprika and parsley and cut into wedges.

TAKEN FROM *THE AMERICAN TABLE* BY RONALD JOHNSON

SUE'S MEATLOAF

1$^1/_2$ pounds ground chuck

3 slices white bread, with crusts

3 slices onion

1$^3/_4$ tsp. salt

1/2 Tbsp. sugar

pepper

a few sprigs parsley

2–3 cups milk

1 egg

pinch of thyme and basil

Crumb bread in blender. Dump into bowl. Blend onion and rest of ingredients except meat. Pour over breadcrumbs and stir until well mixed. Add meat and mix well. Form into loaf. Bake 45 minutes at 375°. Make gravy with drippings. Stir in a little sour cream before serving. Also add 2 tablespoons sugar.

ALFRED'S SWISS STEAK (SERVES 4)

1¹/₂ pounds round steak, cut 1/2 inch thick
1 tsp. salt, or more
1/4 tsp. pepper

1/4 cup flour
3 Tbsp. fat
1 large onion, sliced
stock or beef cubes (optional)

(This is an old Midwest standby and an excellent and simple method to cook inferior beef if you cannot procure the best.) Spread out steak on board. Sprinkle with half the salt, pepper, and flour and pound it all into the steak with wooden meat hammer or heavy frying pan. (This is sometimes a messy job, the flour flying off in all directions unless carefully and firmly managed.) Then turn and pound the remaining flour, salt, and pepper into the other side. The steak should look pale and dry, but if it does not, pound in additional flour. Cut into individual portions and fry in hot fat on both sides until nicely browned, with no blood oozing through. Turn down heat, spread onion slices over top, and cover with hot water. Cover and simmer an hour or two. If water boils down too low, add more. Stock or 2 bouillon cubes dissolved in water make a richer tasting dish, but in the latter case, be careful of salting too highly. The gravy will be thickened enough, so put all on platter and serve.

"IT [DINNER] WAS A LONG ORDEAL. IT WAS PROBABLY A COUPLE OF HOURS, BECAUSE IN BETWEEN EACH ENTRÉE, OR IN BETWEEN THE SALAD, THE MAIN MEAL AND DESSERT, THERE WAS TALK. I MEAN THEY TALKED AND TALKED AND TALKED. I WOULD HAVE TO COME IN AND FIX THE FIRE PROBABLY TWO OR THREE TIMES DURING THE MEAL."

J. SMART (WORKED FOR THE LUNTS IN THE 1970S).
FROM TEN CHIMNEYS FOUNDATION'S ORAL HISTORIES PROJECT

ALFRED'S SZEGED GOULASH (SERVES 4–6)

2 Tbsp. pork drippings (or lard)
1 large onion, chopped
1 Tbsp. mild paprika
1 to 1 1/2 pounds cold roast pork

2–3 cups sauerkraut
1/4 tsp. caraway seeds
salt, very little, if any
1 cup sour cream

If you like sauerkraut, this is a deliciously rich dish, but it may be advisable to serve it only in the country in the middle of a heavy working day. Preheat a kettle and in it melt the pork drippings (or lard). Add the chopped onion and cook until gold in color. Sprinkle in this the paprika; mix well and then add the roast pork cut in 2" to 3" cubes. Stir it around until all is well mixed. Add the sauerkraut and caraway seeds and salt if necessary. If too dry, add water, but not too much–just enough to make it sloppy. Simmer over a very low fire for 1 1/2 hours. Then add the sour cream and simmer for 1/2 hour more and serve with mashed potatoes and a large glass of cold light beer. Another method is to use 1 pound salt pork cut in 1/2" cubes and fried crisp. Take from pan and in the hot fat left, fry an onion until yellow. Pour off fat, add fried pork cubes to onion, then paprika and sauerkraut, and proceed as above.

ALFRED'S VEAL PAPRIKA (SERVES 3)

1/3 cup onions, chopped
2 Tbsp. butter
1 tsp. paprika
1 pound veal, cut in 2- to
    3-inch pieces

1/2 tsp. salt, divided
1 cup consommé
1 1/2 cups water
2 Tbsp. flour
2 Tbsp. water

Cook onions in butter until gold in color. Add paprika, stirring it in well. Then add meat and cook until brownish. Then add 1/4 teaspoon salt, consommé, and water. Simmer for 1 1/2 hours. Then add 1/4 teaspoon salt and thicken with flour and water. One-half cup sour cream may be added. When serving, sprinkle with finely chopped parsley or green pepper, and surround with boiled potatoes, noodles, or potato dumplings.

1 pound veal, cut in 2- to
3-inch pieces
2 cups boiling water

1/2 tsp. salt, divided
small bunch of dill, tied

Put veal in saucepan, pour over boiling water and add 1/4 teaspoon salt and dill. When it comes to a boil, skim. Simmer for 1$^1/_2$ hours. Add water if it evaporates. Remove dill. Pour off stock and keep warm to one side. There should be 1$^1/_2$ cups. In double boiler heat together: 2 tablespoons flour and 2 tablespoons butter. Add stock. Cook until thickened. Add meat, 1/4 teaspoon salt, 2 teaspoons chopped dill, and some white pepper. Serve with boiled potatoes, noodles, or potato dumplings.

ALFRED AND LYNN SITTING OUTSIDE THE POOLHOUSE.

MAIN DISHES

The Lunts strolling the grounds of Ten Chimneys.

ALFRED'S BAKED CHICKEN WITH PARSLEY

3¹/₂ to 4 pounds chicken	1/8 tsp. pepper
1/3 cup fine breadcrumbs	2 Tbsp. butter, or less
3/4 cup parsley, chopped	1 Tbsp. flour, or thickening
1 Tbsp. salt	sauce

Cut up chicken as for fricassee (see page 80) and put a layer in a tightly covered baking dish, then a layer of breadcrumbs and a layer of parsley, some of the salt and pepper, and dot with a little butter. (If the chicken is fat, use no butter at all.) Repeat until ingredients are used up. Pour over 4 cups water, cover, set in 350° oven, and cook for 2¹/₂ hours. Remove chicken and if there is too much fat on liquid, skim some off. Then thicken with 1 tablespoon flour mixed smooth in 1/3 cup water. Return chicken to sauce and serve.

ALFRED'S BOILED CHICKEN AND BACON
(DUBLIN STYLE)

Truss and boil a whole 4-pound chicken, and in a separate pot, boil a 2-pound piece of lean Irish bacon. If not procurable, use Canadian bacon or smoked pork ribs or shank. Arrange sliced hot chicken and bacon on a platter and serve with a separate sauce, either a fricassee (see page 80) sauce made with chicken stock or a thin white sauce. On another platter arrange boiled potatoes, quartered cabbage, carrots (large ones whole) and onions. Do not add butter to vegetables. Be sure everything is very hot.

ALFRED'S BOILED CHICKEN
WITH WHOLE LEMON (SERVES 4-6)

1 stewing hen	1 large bunch parsley
1 large onion	several celery tops
1 lemon	salt and pepper

Sauce:

1 Tbsp. butter	2 Tbsp. flour

Put hen, cut up as for fricassee (see page 80), in kettle and just cover with boiling water. Add onion, parsley, and celery tied in a bunch, a whole lemon, and 2 teaspoons salt. Simmer until tender (2$^1/_2$ hours or more). Remove vegetable bunch and lemon (be sure it does not break) and set meat to one side. Remove fat from liquid, strain and proceed with sauce.

ALFRED'S BROILED BABY TURKEY

Same as Pan-Broiled Chicken. See page 86.

ALFRED'S BROILED DUCKLING (3-4 POUNDS)

Same as Pan-Broiled Chicken (see page 86) but omit butter and pour off fat before adding water to juices. Only very young ducks can be broiled successfully.

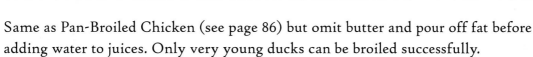

"One thing I remember very vividly was us being workers, how down to earth he was with us. When we were building the creamery, one thing comes to mind. Up past the pool, and all we could see was this bright flashing, and wouldn't you know, here come Jules [the Lunts' butler] with a silver tray with coffee service on it. And the maid with sandwiches, and this was break time. And we never took a break! In those years, you didn't even think of taking a break. It was really something, because they did that every day for us."

F. Plehn (worked for the Lunts),
from Ten Chimneys Foundation's Oral Histories Project

ALFRED'S CHICKEN FRICASSEE WITH HOT BISCUITS
(SERVES 6)

1 stewing chicken	salt and pepper
1 celery stalk	butter and flour, for sauce
1 onion	hot baking powder biscuits

Hair the fowl, cut up, put in kettle with cut-up celery, onion, and 1 teaspoon salt; just cover with water and simmer until done—2 to 3 hours (depends on fowl). Remove chicken, strain broth and remove fat, and proceed to make sauce, making twice the quantity. Arrange pieces of fowl on hot platter, surround with hot biscuits, split and buttered. Pour over sauce and serve. Or serve with cooked rice. Sprinkle with chopped parsley.

ALFRED'S CHICKEN FRICASSEE WITH HORSERADISH SAUCE

Press liquid from 2 or more tablespoons of bottled horseradish through a sieve and add horseradish to fricassee sauce. Add also 1/2 teaspoon sugar, or sauce may taste bitter. Fresh horseradish to taste may be used.

"SO ADDICTED IS LUNT TO HIS OWN CUISINE THAT,

ON THE ROAD, HE AND MISS FONTANNE WON'T MAKE

SO MUCH AS A ONE-NIGHT STOP AT ANY HOTEL THAT

CAN'T OFFER THEM A KITCHENETTE."

COLLIER'S, "THE CHEF'S ROLE," 1933

ALFRED'S CHICKEN IN PINK CREAM & SAUCE

Chicken in Pink Cream:

1/2 pound onions, thinly sliced

2 Tbsp. butter

4 breasts of young chicken

4 legs and thighs of young
    chicken

1 pint heavy cream

1¼ tsp. salt

1/8 tsp. pepper

Sauce for Thickening:

2 Tbsp. butter

2 Tbsp. flour

1 cup hot milk

1½ Tbsp. tomato paste

1/2 tsp. salt

1/8 tsp. white pepper

1/4 tsp. paprika

1 Tbsp. lemon juice

1/2 pound mushrooms, no
    stems, sliced and sautéed
    lightly in butter

Boil sliced onions for three minutes. Drain and then cook them in 2 tablespoons butter (in heavy pot) until transparent (do not brown), on them place the chicken parts, add cream, salt, and pepper. Simmer covered until chicken is soft. While this is cooking, make a sauce with the butter, flour, hot milk, tomato paste, salt, pepper, paprika, and lemon juice. Remove chicken parts (when done) and keep warm, and either strain or put through blender the remaining cream and onion. Return to pot and thicken with the sauce—adding half the sautéed mushrooms and surround with either boiled rice or florets (made of puff paste). If the sauce is not pink enough, add a few drops of red coloring. If you wish a thicker sauce, stir in an egg yolk beaten with a little cream, in which case do not allow it to boil as it will curdle.

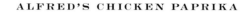

ALFRED'S CHICKEN PAPRIKA

1 to 3 pounds chicken, cut in
    six or more pieces
salt and pepper
4 Tbsp. butter
2 Tbsp. sweet paprika
2 medium onions, thinly
    sliced

1/2 pound mushrooms
1 large green pepper, seeded
    and cut in strips
1 cup chicken broth
1 cup whipping cream

Salt and pepper chicken, then brown in butter, skin-side down. Turn, sprinkle with the paprika. Add onions and sliced mushrooms. Cover pot and cook over medium heat for 20 minutes. Add green pepper strips and hot broth. Re-cover, simmer 15 minutes or until tender. Remove chicken and pepper strips. Keep warm while you add the 1 cup cream to the sauce. Bring to a boil, stirring constantly. Arrange chicken and pepper strips on serving dish. Pour the sauce over this. Sprinkle with finely chopped parsley.

ALFRED'S CHICKEN TARRAGON (SERVES 4)

3 pounds chicken
4 cups chicken broth, or 2
    cups chicken broth and
    2 cups water

1 small onion
fresh or dried tarragon
salt and dash of white
    pepper

Truss the chicken, put it in a pot and pour on hot broth, the sliced onion and a small bunch of fresh tarragon or 1 teaspoon of dried tarragon. Cover and simmer until done, about $1^1/_2$ hours. Take out chicken, strain liquid, and make sauce. Add 1/2 teaspoon chopped fresh, or 1/4 teaspoon dried, tarragon leaves and sprinkle some over chicken when serving. Serve sauce separately but pour a few spoonfuls over chicken before bringing to table.

1/2 cup flour

1 tsp. salt

1/4 tsp. pepper

1 frying chicken, cut up

1/4 pound butter, or more

Chicken can be fried in many kinds of fat: vegetable, chicken or lard, but if fried in butter and smothered it is most tempting.

Sauce:

2 Tbsp. flour

2 cups water or milk

Put flour, salt, and pepper in a paper bag. In this, shake the pieces of chicken, which have been washed and thoroughly dried. Melt the butter in a hot frying pan. There should be at least 1/2 inch of it when melted, and in this, fry the pieces of chicken until golden, turning frequently, being sure they do not burn. Cover, turn heat very low, and let steam until soft and tender, about 30 to 45 minutes. Remove chicken to hot platter and keep warm. Pour off all but 2 tablespoons of butter left in pan. (Strain and save for other fryings.) Stir in 2 tablespoons flour, scraping sides and bottom as it browns, and add 2 cups of hot water or milk. Add a pinch of sugar, and salt and pepper to taste. Strain and serve separately with chicken. Corn pancakes, spoon bread, or corn pudding are assets.

ALFRED'S PAN-BROILED CHICKEN

1 young chicken, 1½ to
2½ pounds
salt and pepper

flour
butter
hot water

Chicken prepared in this manner is moist, rich, and delicious. Wash and dry chicken, cut off neck and split down the back, but do not cut quite in two, so that the bird can be opened but still in one piece. Sprinkle both sides with salt and pepper, and dust lightly with flour. Smear a low baking pan generously with butter and on this lay and spread out the chicken, skin-side down. Dot with more butter. Place 8 inches under preheated broiler. Allow to brown, basting frequently, then turn and brown and baste the other side. Turn again, lower oven to 325° (close door) and let cook for 1 hour, basting every 15 minutes. Remove chicken to platter; keep warm. Set the pan over a burner, add about 1/2 cup hot water to juices, and let simmer 2 minutes. Pour this over chicken and serve. The basting is most important.

ALFRED'S PLAIN ROAST CHICKEN (SERVES 4)

3½ to 4 pounds chicken
2 onions
4 carrots

1/4 cup water
salt and pepper

Wash chicken and dry. Stuff with 1 peeled onion and 2 carrots. Truss. Place in small baking pan and brown in 400° oven. Add 1/4 cup water and remaining onion and carrots. Cover tightly and roast, basting frequently, for about 2 hours. Remove string, carve and serve with thickened juices remaining in pan. If too fat, skim the juice, and if not sufficient in quantity, add clear, strong chicken broth. Discard the vegetables.

ALFRED'S ROASTED CHICKEN BIOT

1/4 pound salt pork, diced in small cubes
1 to 3½ pounds chicken, trussed or at least tied with string to prevent legs and wings from springing out

8 carrots, peeled but left whole
6 medium potatoes or 12 small, peeled
6 medium onions or 12 small, peeled
pepper
salt, only if necessary

Put diced pork in a preheated iron kettle (with a tight-fitting cover) and fry until cubes are "tied out" or crisp. Then remove them from pot and set to one side. In the fat, brown chicken on all sides. Set it also to one side and brown all the vegetables. This should be done over a hot fire but be careful not to burn anything. When vegetables are browned, remove them to one side. Pour all fat from pot. Replace chicken and vegetables. Grind some pepper over all and bake tightly covered for 2½ hours. Remove string from bird. Place on platter and surround with vegetables and serve sauce separately. There should be about 2 cups of clear, natural juices from the bird and vegetables. Do not thicken. Serve with green beans or peas. At one end of platter, place a pile of hot sautéed almonds and at other end a pile of hot stoned prunes. Very nice.

"So if you get an invitation to dine—my tip is DINE—for you do dine well, considering that Alfred always cooks the one dish that is the pièce de résistance of the meal."

ELSA MAXWELL FROM
"ELSA MAXWELL'S WEEKEND ROUND-UP" COLUMN, 1946

SIDE DISHES

POTATOES

Alfred and Lynn harvesting the gardens of Ten Chimneys.

ALFRED LUNT'S
COOKBOOK
TESTER'S EDITION

ANNA'S BAKED POTATOES

3–4 medium-sized potatoes	1/4 pound butter
salt and pepper	

Do not use new potatoes. Peel and slice potatoes very thin. Soak in water for 1 hour. Remove and dry thoroughly; salt and pepper to taste. Smear bottom and sides of a 7" baking or frying pan with butter. Then lay in a layer of potato slices in a circular design—a row around the side. Dot lower layer with butter. Then add layer after layer until pan is full, dotting each layer with butter. Bake in a 375° oven. Turn out on a plate and serve. This can be done in muffin pans and served around steaks, etc.

ALFRED'S BAKED SLICED POTATOES

6 Idaho potatoes, baked and then chilled with their skins on	1 tsp. salt, or to taste
	2 Tbsp. chopped fresh dill
	1 Tbsp. fresh parsley
8 Tbsp. (1 stick) butter	

Preheat the oven to 400°. Slice the potatoes very thin and lay them in a buttered baking dish, each slice slightly overlapping the one next to it. Dot with the butter and sprinkle with salt. Bake until golden brown and crunchy, about 25 to 30 minutes. Sprinkle with chopped dill and parsley.

TAKEN FROM *THE HERITAGE OF SOUTHERN COOKING* BY CAMILLE GLENN

"THE ACTOR, ALFRED LUNT, WHO GAVE ME SOME COOKING LESSONS FOR THE USO IN WASHINGTON, DC, DURING WWII, TAUGHT ME THIS. YOU'LL LOVE THEM. EVERYONE DOES."

CAMILLE GLENN

ALFRED'S CREAMED BAKED POTATOES (SERVES 5–6)

Bake 3 medium-sized potatoes. Put them in refrigerator overnight. Peel, cut into small cubes, and put them in top of double boiler over steaming water. Pour on just enough cream to cover them and let heat in this manner for 3 hours. Stir twice with large tined fork. Season to taste with salt and pepper just before serving.

ALFRED'S CREAMED BOILED POTATOES (SERVES 5–6)

Same as Creamed Baked Potatoes, but add a pinch of mace or nutmeg.

ALFRED'S COUNTRY HASHED POTATOES

This is rather an original way of hash-browning potatoes and has a taste of its own. It requires a special cutter: punch nail holes in the bottom of an emptied, cleaned soup can and be sure the other opened end is smooth because it is this end that is used for chopping, not the end with the punched holes. Preheat iron frying pan, put in a generous amount of butter, and when melted, slice into it cold boiled potatoes already salted and peppered to taste. Then proceed at once to chop potatoes with the opened end of the can, shaking it out to remove pieces that may stick inside. Chop until potatoes are quite fine. Let cook, turning them about now and then, until they have a full, strong, buttery taste. Do not allow to brown, but serve very hot. Awfully good with eggs fried in butter, sausages, toast, currant jelly, and coffee. My Aunt Achsah used to flip eggs into the wood stove fire if the yolk of a frying egg broke in the pan—the men folks wouldn't eat it!

ALFRED'S POTATO PANCAKES

3 medium-sized raw potatoes	1 Tbsp. cream
1 tsp. salt	1 Tbsp. flour
	1 egg, beaten

Grate potatoes. Add salt, cream, flour, and beaten egg. Beat all together well, Heat frying pan, use fat to cover, and drop mixture with a large spoon. Fry, turning with spatula. Cook thoroughly, and be sure they are brown. Serve with pot roast or applesauce.

TAKEN FROM *UNITED NATIONS RECIPES FOR WAR RATIONED COOKING*, P.67

ALFRED'S "FRENCH FRIED" POTATOES IN BUTTER
(SERVES 4)

4 medium potatoes	1/3 cup butter (2 1/2 ounces)

This can be done in a frying pan in the oven or on top of the stove. Peel potatoes and cut into 1/2" strips. Let stand in cold water for 1/2 hour. Drain and dry. Preheat frying pan and melt in it 1/3 cup butter. Add potatoes and stir them carefully so that butter will coat them all. Turn them occasionally and very carefully until done, about 30 minutes. Salt and serve. (Longer if cooked in 375° oven.)

ALFRED'S POTATOES BÄSTADT

3–4 medium-sized potatoes	salt and pepper
3 Tbsp. butter, or 1/2 butter and 1/2 lard or vegetable fat	

Peel and shred potatoes and soak in cold water for 1 or 2 hours. Drain and dry thoroughly. Add "fat" to preheated frying pan and, when melted, add shredded potatoes, salted and peppered to taste. Cook slowly but let brown, turning once or twice during first 10 minutes. Put on cover and cook until soft all through. Turn out whole, on a plate.

PASTAS, RICES, & PUDDINGS

LE CORDON BLEU

Siège Social : **129**, rue du Faubourg-Saint-Honoré

Fondé en 1895 - R. C. Seine 306.414

Téléphone : ÉLYsées 35-39

ACADÉMIE DE CUISINE

DIPLOME DE CUISINE BOURGEOISE ET DE PATISSERIE COURANTE

Délivré à Mʳ *Alfred Lunt*

DEGRÉ

PARIS, le

LES PROFESSEURS :

LA DIRECTRICE :

Ce Diplôme est décerné a tout élève ayant passé un concours oral, pratique et écrit. Pour se présenter aux examens des Diplômes supérieurs ce premier Diplôme sera demandé.

ALFRED'S DIPLOMA FROM LE CORDON BLEU STILL HANGS IN THE MAIN HOUSE KITCHEN OF TEN CHIMNEYS.

ALFRED LUNT'S

COOKBOOK

TESTER'S EDITION

© TCF

ALFRED'S BOILED RICE

THERE ARE MANY METHODS OF COOKING RICE, BUT THIS RECIPE IS
AS SIMPLE AND ABOUT AS SATISFACTORY AS YOU WILL FIND.

1 cup long-grained Carolina rice	2½ cups boiling water salt

Wash rice thoroughly, using several waters. Drain and gradually add to boiling salted water in double boiler top, over direct heat, and boil 5 minutes. Then place over lower part of double boiler, cover and steam for 40 minutes or until water is absorbed and rice is tender. Handle with a fork.

ALFRED'S DIRTY RICE (SERVES 4)
(THE NAME IS MISLEADING)

2 Tbsp. butter	1/4 pound chopped
1/4 cup chopped celery	mushrooms
1/4 cup chopped onions	1 cup cooked long-grained
1/4 cup chopped green	Carolina rice
peppers	salt and pepper

Melt the butter in a preheated frying pan. Add the chopped vegetables and fry until light brown. Stir in the cooked rice with a fork, mixing well. Add salt and pepper to taste. Heat thoroughly and serve.

ALFRED'S EGG BARLEY (OR TARBONYA)

2 Tbsp. butter

1 to 1½ tsp. onion, chopped

1 cup egg barley

1½ to 2 cups water, boiling

Heat butter in a heavy skillet. Add chopped onions and fry until yellow. Stir in the egg barley and brown. Add boiling water and cook slowly until soft. Salt and pepper to taste. Cover and keep over low heat or in top of double boiler or in the oven. Stir occasionally with a large fork to keep kernels separate. Serve in place of potatoes or noodles with any paprika dish.

ALFRED'S FETTUCCINE

8 ounces medium-sized noodles

1/2 stick butter

1/2 pint sour cream

1/2 pint heavy cream

1/2 cup parmesan cheese, grated

sprinkling of nutmeg

salt and pepper, to taste

2 tsp. chives, finely chopped

Cook noodles. Drain. Melt butter in heavy pan and add noodles. Add sour cream, stirring a minute or two over a low flame. Add heavy cream and cook slowly for a few minutes. Add cheese, nutmeg, salt and pepper, and half the chives and continue stirring until cheese is melted. Serve sprinkled with remaining chives.

"I'M JUST A COUNTRY BOY WHO HAPPENS TO BE AN ACTOR. BUT FASHIONABLE PARTIES AND CLEVER TALK—ALL THAT SORT OF THING—WELL YA KNOW IT BORES ME STIFF. I'D RATHER LISTEN TO MY HENS CLUCKING ANYTIME."

ALFRED LUNT

ALFRED'S NOODLES ALFREDO (FETTUCCINE)
(SERVES 4–5)

6 ounces noodles
1/3 cup butter
1/2 cup cream

1/3 cup parmesan cheese, grated

Boil noodles in slightly salted water until done. Drain and rinse in cold water. Melt butter in pan; add cream and then grated cheese. Add noodles. Heat thoroughly. Salt to taste. When serving, sprinkle with chopped parsley.

ALFRED'S FISH PUDDING (SERVES 4)

2 cups water
1/2 tsp. salt
1 small onion
a few celery tops with leaves
3 sprigs parsley
1/2 pound haddock, fresh
    or frozen

2 Tbsp. butter
3 Tbsp. flour
$1^1/_2$ cups milk, scant
2 eggs, separated
pepper

To 2 cups water, add salt, onion, celery tips, and parsley. Let boil 5 minutes; then add fish and simmer 15 minutes. Remove fish and set it aside; strain liquor and save. Flake fish. In skillet, melt 2 tablespoons butter; add 3 tablespoons flour, and then whisk in hot milk and 1/4 cup hot fish liquor. This must be thick. Add flaked fish and egg yolks and fold in the stiffly beaten egg whites. Put in a buttered casserole and bake 1 hour in 375° oven. Serve with sauce—separately.

Sauce:

2 Tbsp. butter
2 Tbsp. flour
3/4 cup hot milk
1/4 cup hot fish liquor

1 Tbsp. sour cream
salt and white pepper
fresh dill, chopped,
    if possible

Melt butter; whisk in flour, then milk and fish liquor. Whisk until smooth. Add sour cream, salt and pepper to taste and chopped dill to taste.

ALFRED'S PILAF

3 Tbsp. butter

2 medium onions, finely
chopped

1 cup rice

2 cups hot water or stock

Heat butter in heavy pot (with a lid that fits snuggly). Add onions and cook but do not color. Stir in the rice and, when butter is absorbed, add the hot water (or stock). Stir. Bring to a boil. Cover and bake in a 425° oven for 20 minutes. Remove from oven and keep covered until ready to serve. You can omit the onions and instead brown the rice in the butter and proceed as above.

ALFRED'S RED RICE

2 Tbsp. butter

1/3 cup onion, chopped

1/3 cup celery, chopped

1/3 cup green pepper, chopped

5–6 medium-sized tomatoes,
peeled

salt and pepper

1 cup uncooked rice

Tabasco sauce (optional)

Heat the butter in preheated frying pan. Add the chopped vegetables and fry until golden in color. Add the tomatoes, cut up. (There should be enough tomato to make $2\frac{1}{4}$ cups sauce.) Cook all together until done. Add salt and pepper to taste. Then add the dry rice, stirring it in with a fork. Mix thoroughly; cover and let steam over a low fire until thoroughly cooked. Add more salt and pepper if needed and a few drops of Tabasco.

ALFRED'S RICE PUDDING
(OLD-FASHIONED AND VERY GOOD)

1 quart milk	1/2 cup sugar
1/4 cup long grain rice	pinch of salt

Butter bottom and sides of a 6-cup casserole. Pour in the milk and then stir in the rice, the sugar, and the pinch of salt. Set in a slow oven, 300°, until it begins to boil (about one hour). Reduce heat to 275°. Stir occasionally, mixing the crust that may form. Cook until it takes on the consistency of a boiled custard and is slightly sticky. Serve (in the casserole) either hot or cold. The stirring in of "the crust" is a question of personal or family taste.

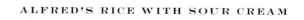

ALFRED'S RICE WITH SOUR CREAM

Fill a small baking dish with cold boiled rice. Over this, pour sour cream (with a little salt) until dish is full. Bake in 375° oven until light brown on top.

ALFRED'S RISOTTO

2 Tbsp. fat, butter or butter and margarine mixed	1 cup rice
	3–4 cups hot stock
3 onions, sliced	salt, to taste

Preheat large iron frying pan. Add butter and, when melted, add onion slices; remove when brown. Then pour in dry rice and stir with a wooden spoon until browned. Add hot stock little by little, stirring constantly until rice has absorbed as much as it will take. It should be very moist, tender but not sloppy. Place in top of double boiler to keep warm.

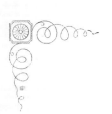

ALFRED'S YORKSHIRE PUDDING (SERVES 6)

THIS IS A GENUINE ENGLISH "BATTER PUDDING," MORE MOIST
THAN THE POPOVER TYPE TO WHICH WE IN THE UNITED STATES
ARE ACCUSTOMED. IT IS USED IN MAKING "TOAD-IN-THE-HOLE."
IN YORKSHIRE, THE BATTER PUDDING IS SERVED BEFORE THE
ROAST TO DAMPEN THE APPETITE FOR THE MEAT.

2 eggs
2 cups milk
2 cups flour, unsifted

1/4 tsp. salt
2 Tbsp. drippings, the clear
    melted fat from roast
    beef

Beat eggs and milk together and stir this gradually into flour and salt which has been
sifted into mixing bowl. Beat for 10 minutes. (I'd advise an electric beater.) Let stand
one hour. Heat drippings until very hot in 7" x 11" pan. Pour into this the batter (which
has been given a few extra last minute beats). Better set pan on large piece of paper as
fat sometimes spills over when batter is added. Bake in 450° oven for 10 minutes, and
then lower oven to 350° and bake 15 minutes longer. Cut into large pieces and serve
around roast beef.

SIDE DISHES

VEGETABLES

ALFRED PRESENTS HIS HOMEGROWN
TREASURES.

ALFRED LUNT'S
COOKBOOK
TESTER'S EDITION

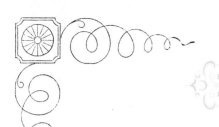

ALFRED'S CORN PUDDING

1 can corn, cream style	1½ cups milk
3 Tbsp. flour	2 eggs
1/2 tsp. salt and white pepper	butter

Mash the corn through a sieve and stir into it the flour, salt, pepper, milk, and eggs. Mix thoroughly. Pour into buttered casserole. Set in a pan of water and bake in a 350° oven for [left untyped in original manuscript]. Serve at once. This should not curdle.

ALFRED'S BAKED EGGPLANT AND TOMATOES
(SERVES 6)

1 smallish eggplant	breadcrumbs
4 tomatoes, peeled	butter
salt and pepper	

Peel the eggplant and cut in 1/2" slices. Sprinkle each piece with a little salt. Place one on the other, and place a plate and weight on top. Let stand a few hours. Place them in rows in a shallow pan, the bottom of which is lightly smeared with butter, and carefully salt and pepper each one. Over these, place a slice of tomato 1/2" thick. If the sizes are equal, so much the better. Sprinkle with salt, pepper, and then breadcrumbs, and put a small lump of butter on top of all. Bake in 350° oven for 1 hour or until soft and brown.

ALFRED'S CABBAGE

1 small head of cabbage   milk or sour cream
caraway seeds, optional

Shave 1/2 (unless very small) head of cabbage in very thin slices. Put in salted boiling water. Cook 13 minutes. Drain. Put in top of double boiler and add salt, pepper, and a small bag of caraway seeds. Cover with milk or sour cream. Keep hot for not less than 1/2 hour, stirring occasionally. (A version of this recipe also appeared on page 70 of the *United Nations Recipes for War Rationed Cooking*.)

ALFRED'S CARROTS

Young carrots, well scrubbed, leaving on 1/2" of their stems, pressure cooked for 3 minutes are delicious. The stems are attractive though not eaten.

ALFRED'S CARROTS AND MINT

Add chopped fresh mint leaves to cooked carrots.

ALFRED'S CELERY

When using large, full-grown celery, cut off leaves, and, with a very sharp knife, pare off the stringy outside. (Save the parings and leaves for soup or sauces.) Cut in pieces and cook and serve in a cream sauce, or however you wish.

ALFRED'S CREAMED FRESH GREEN CORN
(SERVES 4)

6 ears corn
1/8 tsp. salt
1/2 tsp. sugar

1 Tbsp. butter
milk

Shave kernels off young corncobs, being sure to scrape out all milk. Put in small saucepan and add 1/8 teaspoon salt, or to taste, 1/2 teaspoon sugar, and 1 tablespoon butter; just cover with milk. Cook slowly until done—from 8 to 15 minutes.

ALFRED'S FILLED CABBAGE ROLLS

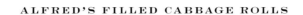

1 medium-sized cabbage	1/2 cup milk
1/4 pound ground beef	1 egg
1/4 pound ground pork	3 Tbsp. butter
1 cup cooked rice	1 Tbsp. brown sugar
1/2 tsp. salt	1 tsp. tarragon vinegar
1/4 tsp. freshly ground pepper	2 cups stock or water

Sauce:

1 Tbsp. flour	1/2 cup cream or top milk

Discard the outer leaves of cabbage and cut out the core. Then remove the large leaves, taking care not to tear. Wilt them in boiling salted water (2 teaspoons salt to 1 quart water) until pliable. Drain. Or immerse whole cored cabbage in boiling water until leaves separate easily. Wilt as above. When drained, trim out hard center vein.

Filling:

To the ground beef and pork add cooked rice, salt, and pepper, and then the milk beaten with the egg. Stir well. It should be the consistency of thick mush. Add 2 tablespoons of this to each cabbage leaf. Roll, folding in sides, and either tie with string or use toothpicks to keep them in shape. Brown on all sides in the melted butter in the baking dish, and this, by the way, will take some time. When brown, sprinkle on the brown sugar and tarragon vinegar. Add stock. Cover and bake in 350° oven for $1\frac{1}{2}$ hours. Remove cabbage roll. Thicken juices in pan with 1 tablespoon flour mixed with milk or cream. Strain over cabbage rolls (string or toothpicks removed), and serve. Good with mashed or plain boiled potatoes.

ALFRED'S GREEN BEANS/WAX BEANS

Cook, salt and pepper, and lay in straight bundles or in rows with a quantity of melted butter poured over, just to give them a sheen, and sprinkle with very fine parsley or buttered breadcrumbs.

ALFRED'S SPINACH

Is there anything more unappetizing than a dish of black spinach swimming in swamp water? It need not be so. Spinach must be washed three or four times, or until no grit remains on the leaves. Put in a pot and cook in the moisture left from washing. Pile it high in the pot if need be as it collapses into less than you plan. Then drain it, pressing it down hard. Drink the juice in private. Season after cooking with butter, salt, and pepper. It will be an emerald green if not left in pot too long.

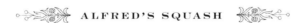

ALFRED'S SQUASH

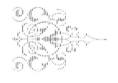

There are infinite ways of cooking our many varieties of squash. Here are a few recipes. Proportions are difficult to determine as so much depends on size of squash.

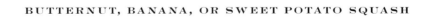

BUTTERNUT, BANANA, OR SWEET POTATO SQUASH

Peel squash, split lengthwise, and remove seeds. Slice in 2" pieces. Place in rows in shallow baking tin, sprinkle with salt to taste and brown sugar. Add lumps of butter and bake in a 350° oven for about 1 hour. Baste frequently.

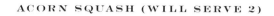

ACORN SQUASH (WILL SERVE 2)

Cut in two and sprinkle inside with salt (and a little brown or white sugar, if desired). Bake in 375° oven for 1 hour. Put in piece of butter. Eat from shell or remove and mash with butter.

CROOKED NECK OR STRAIGHT NECK SQUASH

If very young, cut away 1" from each end. Slice and boil in salted water to cover until soft. Drain off water and return to pot; mash, salt and pepper, add some butter, and "cook down" until not too watery. Half an onion diced and sautéed can be added before mashing. If squash is old and large, it is best peeled and seeded; otherwise, it will taste and have the texture of cardboard.

ALFRED'S ZUCCHINI

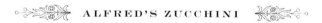

BLACK GREEN OR GRAYISH GREEN VARIETIES

If small, 3–4", boil whole or split in two in salted water, just enough to cover. They are best underdone. Serve with melted or browned butter and salt and pepper to taste. Or, if 5" or larger, slice and fry in olive oil or butter, or dust with flour, salt, and pepper and fry in deep fat. Or, if very large, 1 foot or more, peel, remove seeds, slice in 2" pieces, and boil in salted water. Serve with a white sauce or melted butter as you would English marrow.

WHITE SCALLOPED VARIETY

If very small, cook whole in salted water and serve with melted butter and salt and pepper to taste. Best underdone. If 2" to 3", split, parboil gently, drain, set in shallow pan, salt and pepper, and sprinkle with breadcrumbs. Dot with butter, and broil or bake in 375° oven until browned.

Split large ones, 4" or more, the wide way. Remove seeds and parboil; scrape out and mix pulp with pepper, salt, and some onion juice. Replace in shells, cover with breadcrumbs, dot with butter, and broil or bake. Crooked neck, straight neck and white scalloped varieties can be peeled, seeded, cut up, and boiled down in a small quantity of salted water, put in casserole, sprinkled with breadcrumbs, dotted with butter, and baked. All the yellow varieties, such as the butternut, acorn, and hubbard, can be baked, the pulp scraped out, and to that added salt, pepper to taste, brown sugar, or a little cream, beaten up well, and served as you would mashed potatoes.

ALFRED'S PEAS

4 cups water

1 tsp. salt

1 Tbsp. sugar

pinch of soda

1 pound green peas, shelled

Peas must be watched and tasted constantly while cooking. Have water boiling in pot (to which you have added salt, sugar, and soda). Pour in peas and if the water more than covers them, remove some—water, not peas. Boil softly and taste after 5 minutes. When done, they will pop between your front teeth. Drain if too much water is left, and add butter or cream—no pepper. If peas are oldish, add a few sprigs of mint while cooking.

ALFRED'S SLICED CUCUMBERS

1 cucumber, medium-sized

1 tsp. vinegar

1/2 tsp. salt

1 Tbsp. sugar

dash of white pepper

1 Tbsp. fresh parsley or dill,
    chopped

Peel cucumber and slice very thin. Put in bowl and mix thoroughly with salt. Let stand 1/2 hour and then press off liquid. Now mix in sugar, vinegar and chopped parsley or dill; let stand 1/2 hour in icebox. Cucumbers so prepared may look a bit limp and untidy but are digestible and an addition to any summer luncheon or dinner. Another way is to slice a cucumber without peeling. Marinate it in the vinegar, salt, sugar, and pepper, and then arrange on a plate in rows, each slice overlapping.

CUCUMBER WITH SOUR CREAM

Same as in Cucumber recipe, adding 1/2 teaspoon finely chopped onion and 1/2 cup sour cream.

ALFRED'S GRILLED OR BAKED TOMATOES

2 medium-sized tomatoes

salt and pepper

sugar

onion juice

bread or cracker crumbs

butter

The proportions are approximate. Peel (or not as you wish) the tomatoes; cut in half, and place on baking dish, cut side up. If they won't stand, slice a little piece off bottom. Over each surface, grind some pepper and sprinkle 1/4 teaspoon salt, 1/2 teaspoon sugar, and 1/8 teaspoon onion juice. Cover with breadcrumbs and top with a piece of butter the size of a hazelnut. Broil or bake (400° oven) until brown and cooked through.

ALFRED'S LEEKS

Cut about 5" or 6" in length. Peel, simmer in salted water, drain, and serve with hot cream, salted slightly, poured over them.

"AH, AND WHAT ELSE DID WE HAVE? ZUCCHINI. I REMEMBER HE HAD ZUCCHINI QUITE A BIT, AND, AH, A LOT OF THINGS FROM THE GARDEN. GREEN BEANS, HE LOVED. I MEAN GREEN BEANS WERE ONE OF HIS FAVORITE VEGETABLES, I WOULD THINK."

**J. SMART (WORKED FOR THE LUNTS IN THE 1970S),
FROM TEN CHIMNEYS FOUNDATION'S ORAL HISTORIES PROJECT**

ALFRED'S MUSHROOM PAPRIKA

1 pound mushrooms	1/4 tsp. salt
2 Tbsp. butter	flour
1/2 to 1 tsp. paprika	2/3 cup sweet or sour cream

Peel and remove stems of mushrooms. Preheat frying pan. Add butter, and when melted, add mushrooms and cook covered, stirring occasionally, until soft, but not quite done. Sprinkle with paprika and salt; stir. Then sprinkle with flour, just enough to hold the mass together. Add cream and simmer for 5 to 10 minutes. More salt can be added to taste.

Alfred's Tips:

TO CAN TOMATOES WHOLE

Peel well-shaped tomatoes, remove hard green core, and fit them carefully into wide-mouthed quart jars. Fill jars with juice made from skins, cores, and unshapely tomatoes, strained. (Drink any left over.) Add 1 teaspoon salt to each jar. Seal tightly. Put jars in large kettle (on rack to keep them from cracking), pour over hot water, bring to boil, and boil for 20 minutes covered. Leave in kettle until room temperature. Remove jars and keep in cool place.

"USUALLY THREE VEGETABLES WERE ON THE DAILY MENU. MISS FONTANNE MAINTAINED HER WEIGHT EASILY; SHE SOMETIMES ADDED A BAKED POTATO AS AN EXTRA VEGETABLE TO ADD CALORIES."

WISCONSIN STATE HISTORICAL SOCIETY, "HOME LIFE WITH THE LUNTS" BY CAROLYN EVERY, 1983

Alfred's Tips:

DINNER VEGETABLES

For dinner, here's the trick: Boil vegetables in the double boiler tops; when tender, drain and season; then put over the lower sections to stay at serving temperature. Don't fill the lowers too full of water, though. It's the steam that does the work.

TAKEN FROM "HE LIKES TO COOK," *BETTER HOMES & GARDENS*, AUGUST 1962

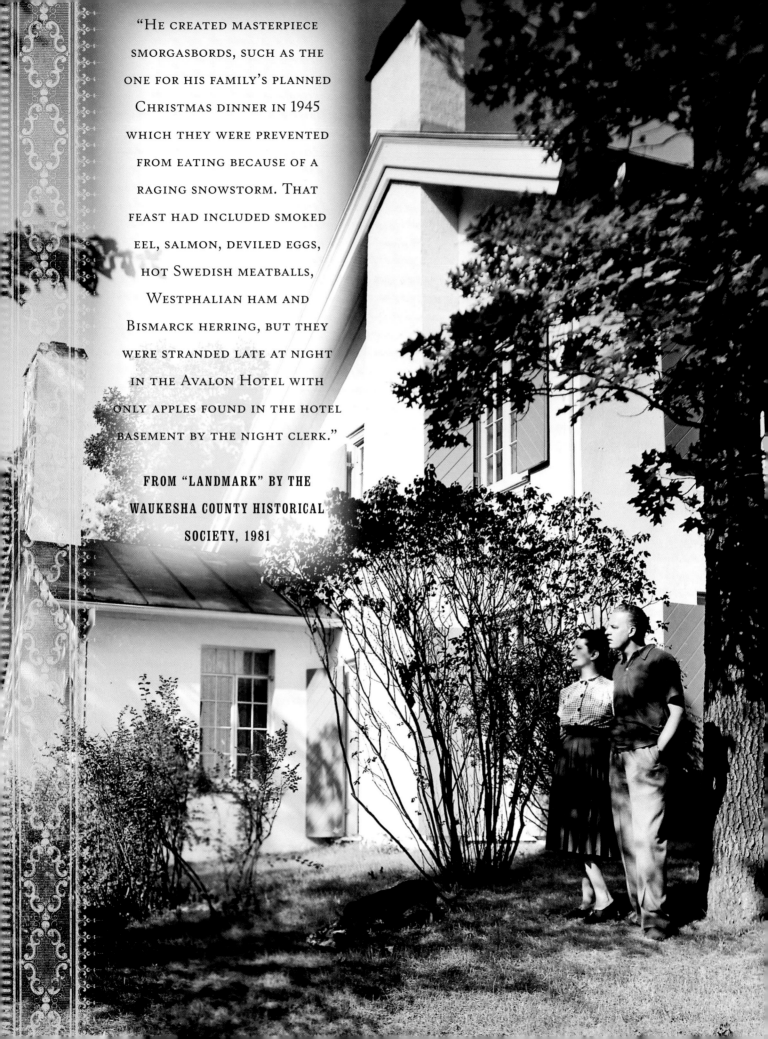

"HE CREATED MASTERPIECE SMORGASBORDS, SUCH AS THE ONE FOR HIS FAMILY'S PLANNED CHRISTMAS DINNER IN 1945 WHICH THEY WERE PREVENTED FROM EATING BECAUSE OF A RAGING SNOWSTORM. THAT FEAST HAD INCLUDED SMOKED EEL, SALMON, DEVILED EGGS, HOT SWEDISH MEATBALLS, WESTPHALIAN HAM AND BISMARCK HERRING, BUT THEY WERE STRANDED LATE AT NIGHT IN THE AVALON HOTEL WITH ONLY APPLES FOUND IN THE HOTEL BASEMENT BY THE NIGHT CLERK."

FROM "LANDMARK" BY THE WAUKESHA COUNTY HISTORICAL SOCIETY, 1981

BREADS

Alfred Lunt in one of his favorite places:
the chef-friendly kitchen of Ten Chimneys.

ALFRED LUNT'S
COOKBOOK
TESTER'S EDITION

ALFRED'S CARDAMOM BREAD
(A TEN CHIMNEYS FOUNDATION FAVORITE)

1 cup milk, scalded	2 pkgs. yeast
18 ground cardamom seeds	1/2 cup warm water
3/4 cup sugar	2 cups flour
2 Tbsp. butter	cinnamon and sugar
2 beaten eggs	1 beaten egg for egg wash

To scalded milk, add the ground cardamom seeds, sugar, and butter. Mix. Add eggs and yeast (that has been softened in the 1/2 cup warm water). Beat well. Add flour (may use more than 2 cups if needed) to make a slightly sticky dough. Grease dough. Let rise until double. Cut down. Let rise one hour. Make into braids in cinnamon and sugar. Let rise again. Bake on a cookie sheet at 350° for 40 minutes. Brush with beaten egg and return to oven for another 25 minutes.

ALFRED'S BREAD

2 cups milk, scalded	3 Tbsp. sugar, divided
4 Tbsp. butter	1 ounce yeast
1 Tbsp. salt	6 cups flour

Heat the milk; when hot, add butter, salt, and 1 tablespoon sugar. Cool and when lukewarm, add to it the yeast, which has been stirred in 2 tablespoons of sugar until liquefied. Gradually stir in as much of the flour as you can and knead in the rest. Place dough on lightly floured board and continue kneading until it is elastic and no longer sticks. Then place it in a lightly buttered bowl; rub a little butter over dough, and cover with a clean cloth. Place in a warm corner and let rise until doubled in bulk 2 to 2$\frac{1}{2}$ hours. Punch down and form into 2 loaves and press them into buttered 8$\frac{1}{2}$" x 4$\frac{1}{2}$" bread pans. Again let rise until doubled in bulk. Bake in a 375° oven for 1 hour. Remove from pans onto a wire rack and cover with a clean cloth if you wish a soft crust, or uncovered if you wish it fairly crisp.

"SOMETIMES AFTER THE THEATRE AT NIGHT HE MADE A BATCH OF BREAD."

WISCONSIN STATE HISTORICAL SOCIETY,

"HOME LIFE WITH THE LUNTS" BY CAROLYN EVERY, 1983

ALFRED'S BUTTERMILK PANCAKES

1 cup cake flour, sift before
measuring

1 tsp. sugar

1/2 tsp. salt

3/4 tsp. baking powder

1/2 tsp. baking soda

1 egg, beaten light

1 cup buttermilk

2 Tbsp. melted butter

Resift flour with sugar, salt, baking powder, and soda. Add this to the mixture of the beaten egg, buttermilk, and melted butter. Add the dry mixture to the wet mixture slowly and only until blended. Do not beat.

ALFRED'S CORN PANCAKES

1 No. 2 (2-cup can) corn,
cream style

2 eggs, separated

3 Tbsp. flour

3 Tbsp. milk

1/2 tsp. salt

Strain corn through a sieve. Stir into it the egg yolks, flour, milk, and salt; lastly, fold in the stiffly beaten egg whites. Drop by spoonfuls onto a hot buttered griddle or iron frying pan to form small pancakes, 2" in diameter. Brown on both sides, turning as you would large pancakes. Serve in piles of 4 or 5 around fried, roasted, or sautéed chicken.

ALFRED'S GRAHAM BREAD

1 cake yeast	1/4 cup molasses
3/4 cup water	1 Tbsp. salt
1 cup milk, scalded	2$\frac{1}{4}$ cups graham flour
1/4 cup shortening	2–3 cups all-purpose flour

Soften compressed yeast in lukewarm water (Or substitute dry yeast and soften in very warm, not hot water). Combine milk, shortening, molasses, and salt in large bowl. Stir to blend. Cool to lukewarm. Add the softened yeast. Add the wheat graham flour; beat well. Gradually add the all-purpose flour, beating after each addition, to form a dough. Knead on floured surface until smooth and satiny, about 10 minutes. Place in greased bowl and cover. Let rise in warm place (85° to 90°) until light and doubled in size, about 2 hours. Punch down dough, cover and let rise again, about 1/2 hour. Divide into four parts. Shape into balls. Cover and let stand for 10 minutes. Shape into 2 loaves and place in well-greased 9 x 5 x 3 inch pans; cover. Let rise until light and doubled in size, about 1 hour. Bake 35–40 minutes in a 375° oven.

ALFRED'S MAPLE SYRUP DUMPLINGS
("DANGEROUS BUT GOOD")

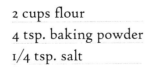

2 cups flour	1/2 cup water
4 tsp. baking powder	1$\frac{1}{2}$ pints maple syrup
1/4 tsp. salt	

Sift flour, baking powder, and salt, and then stir in the water and mix into a smooth batter. Drop by spoonfuls into boiling syrup; cover and cook 15 minutes. Serve with the hot syrup poured over dumplings. Whipped cream may be served with these if you feel up to it.

ALFRED'S SPOON BREAD (SERVES 4–6)

1 cup white, water-ground cornmeal	2 eggs, slightly beaten
	Butter, size of an egg
1 cup boiling water	1/2 tsp. salt
1 cup milk	4 tsp. baking powder

Scald cornmeal with boiling water in a narrow deep bowl. Stir slowly so as not to cool quickly. Add milk, the slightly beaten eggs, and the butter, melted and cooled; then add the salt and baking powder. Pour in a hot baking dish that has been buttered, and bake in a 375° oven for 20 to 25 minutes.

ALFRED'S BUCKWHEAT GRIDDLE CAKES

2 cups boiling water	1 tsp. salt
1/2 ounce yeast	1 tsp. sugar
2 Tbsp. warm water	1/4 tsp. soda
1 1/2 cups buckwheat flour	2 Tbsp. molasses
1/2 cup white flour	1/4 cup lukewarm water

Boil 2 cups of water and, while it is cooling in a bowl, dissolve yeast in 2 tablespoons warm water. Then add to lukewarm water in bowl. Stir in this the flour, salt, and sugar. Cover and keep warm overnight. In the morning, stir in the soda and molasses dissolved in 1/4 cup lukewarm water. Fry like any other griddle cake.

ALFRED'S QUICK BUCKWHEAT GRIDDLE CAKES

2/3 cup buckwheat flour
1/3 cup white flour
1 tsp. baking powder
1/2 tsp. salt
1/2 tsp. soda

1 tsp. sugar
1 cup buttermilk
1 egg, slightly beaten
1 tsp. melted butter
1 tsp. molasses

Mix and sift dry ingredients. Add milk slowly, then beaten egg and beat smooth. Add melted butter and molasses and beat again. Fry like any other griddle cake. If too thick, add more liquid.

ALFRED'S CHEESE BREAD

1/2 cup milk, heated
1/2 cup boiling water
1 Tbsp. butter
$1^1/_4$ tsp. salt
1 tsp. sugar
3/4 cup shredded Cheddar cheese, pressed down in cup

1/4 cup grated Parmesan cheese
1 ounce yeast
1/4 cup warm water
3 cups sifted flour

Add to the hot milk the 1/2 cup boiling water, butter, salt, sugar, and the cheeses. When all is thoroughly combined and the cheese is melted, pour into a bowl. When lukewarm, add the yeast, which has been dissolved in the 1/4 cup of lukewarm water. Then stir in the flour, a little at a time. Knead this dough for 4 or 5 minutes. Let rise until doubled in bulk. Shape into two loaves. Place in small buttered bread tins ($3^1/_2$ x $7^1/_2$) and bake in a 350° oven for 40 minutes.

ALFRED'S EGG DUMPLINGS

1 cup flour, sifted before measuring

1¹/₂ tsp. baking powder

1/2 tsp. salt

1 egg, slightly beaten

1/4 cup plus 2 Tbsp. milk

2 Tbsp. melted butter

Sift together dry ingredients and slowly add to egg, milk, and butter mixture using as few strokes as possible. Drop in largish spoonfuls onto gently boiling stew—letting them rest on the meat. Cover for 15 minutes; then remove cover and let cook another 5 minutes.

ALFRED AND LYNN PLAYING CARDS IN THE GARDEN TERRACE ROOM.

ALFRED'S LIMPA

3/4 cup water	$1\frac{1}{4}$ cups white flour
$1\frac{1}{2}$ Tbsp. molasses	1/2 tsp. anise seed, powdered
2 Tbsp. sugar	1/2 tsp. fennel, powdered
3/4 Tbsp. salt	1/2 of an orange, grated
1 Tbsp. butter	$1\frac{1}{4}$ cups rye flour
1/2 ounce yeast	

Heat water, molasses, sugar, salt, and butter, and when well dissolved, cool to lukewarm and add yeast. Mix well. Then stir in white flour, anise, fennel, and grated orange. Then add rye flour and stir until able to knead. Knead for 5 to 8 minutes. Replace in bowl. Cover with cloth and let rise until doubled in bulk. Push down and let rise again. Form into a round loaf; place on a lightly buttered pie tin. Cover with cloth. Again it should rise until doubled in bulk. Bake in 375° oven for 15 minutes, then 350° for 35 minutes. Remove and rub with a little butter. Put into cloth, then into a plastic bag. Wrap this in a small blanket or an old (clean) sweater and let it cool for 2 hours. Unwrap.

ALFRED'S POTATO DUMPLINGS (MAKES 12)

1 pound potatoes (3 medium-sized)

Boil in jackets and leave in icebox overnight. Peel and either mash thoroughly or put through ricer (or both). There will be $1\frac{1}{2}$ cups, or should be. Add to potatoes: 1 egg, 3/4 teaspoon salt, scant 1/2 cup flour, and grated nutmeg (optional). Mix thoroughly. Shape into balls, 1" or so in diameter, and put a crouton in center of each. Cook in boiling water 10 minutes. Try one first and if it falls apart, add a little more flour. Serve either plain with goulash, pot roast, or veal stew, or with browned butter poured over them. Makes 12.

DESSERTS

ALFRED LUNT AND LYNN FONTANNE ON THE
MAIN HOUSE TERRACE OF TEN CHIMNEYS.

ALFRED'S RUM PUDDING AND SAUCE

4 cups milk	4 Tbsp. cornstarch
1 cup sugar	4 egg yolks

Cook in double boiler.

vanilla or rum	2 egg whites, beaten
1 env. gelatin	1 pint cream
1/2 cup cold water	

When well cooked, add 1 teaspoon vanilla or 4 tablespoons rum. Divide in two parts and to one half, add 1 envelope of gelatin dissolved in 1/2 cup cold water. Cool, and add the beaten whites of 2 eggs. When cold, add 1 pint of cream, whipped. Put into mold and let stand several hours. Serve with other half of custard poured over.

ALFRED'S CARAMEL CUSTARD

Same as Baked Custard (see page 126) except coat bottom and sides of baking dish with the following: 1 cup sugar and 3 tablespoons boiling water. Melt sugar in frying pan until golden in color; add hot water and stir constantly until a syrup is formed. Pour this into baking dish and move it around and about quickly until all sides are covered. When cool, pour in custard and bake in pan of hot water, 325° oven. Unmold onto a shallow bowl. Decorate top with split whole-blanched almonds.

ALFRED'S CANARY PUDDING (STEAMED)

2 eggs

Their weight in butter,
  sugar, and flour

3/4 tsp. baking powder,
  sifted with flour

grated rind of lemon

Cream butter, and thoroughly beat in sugar and grated rind. Beat in a spoonful of flour with the eggs (one at a time); then fold in remaining flour. Turn into well-buttered steamer. Cover, and steam it for $1^{1}/_{2}$ to 2 hours. Remove to dish and serve with a lemon sauce.

ALFRED'S BOILED CUSTARD—VANILLA SAUCE

2 Tbsp. sugar

1 Tbsp. cornstarch

pinch of salt

2 egg yolks

2 cups hot milk

1/4 tsp. vanilla extract

1/4 tsp. almond extract

Mix sugar, cornstarch, salt, and egg yolks in top of double boiler; add scalded milk gradually. Place over lower part of double boiler and cook, stirring constantly until thick or it coats spoon. Cool and add flavoring. If mixture becomes too thick while cooling, beat in 2 tablespoons cold milk. One-half cup of cream, whipped, may be folded in, in which case, add extra 1/2 teaspoon vanilla. This method of using cornstarch in making a soft custard is less nerve-racking than the method of using only eggs—which is apt to curdle. And, by the way, if when pouring hot liquid onto dry materials, you will place the double boiler close to table or stove edge with handles pressed to right hip, while stirring from left to right, you will avoid the inconvenience of the pot whirling around.

ALFRED'S BAKED CUSTARD

3 or 4 eggs	1/4 tsp. vanilla, or a little
3 Tbsp. sugar	grated nutmeg
pinch of salt	cinnamon
3 cups milk	

Beat eggs, sugar, salt, and milk thoroughly. Add seasoning. Pour into buttered baking dish and bake in 325° oven for 40 minutes or until firm. Test by piercing with knife. If blade comes out clean, custard is done. If overcooked, custard will be watery.

ALFRED'S JELLIED STRAWBERRY RING (SERVES 8)

4 cups strawberry syrup	1/2 cup water
2 Tbsp. gelatin	

Heat syrup, and add gelatin dissolved in 1/2 cup water. Simmer a minute or two. Pour into a six-cup mold and keep in icebox until set. Unmold on serving dish; fill with fresh strawberries or whipped cream, or with strawberries in center and mounds of whipped cream around edge.

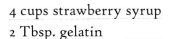

Strawberry Syrup:

4–5 quarts strawberries	sugar

Put hulled strawberries in kettle. Add 1 cup water; cover and heat through. Strain through a thin cloth. To each cup of juice, add 3/4 cup sugar. Put in kettle and boil one minute. Remove all scum and bottle hot.

"ALFRED PUT HIS ARM AROUND NOËL TO COMFORT HIM AND TOLD HIM THAT THEY
WERE SPECIALLY MAKING HIM HIS FAVORITE CHOCOLATE CAKE AS A FIRST-NIGHT
PRESENT ON THE MORROW. NOËL UNDERSTOOD COMPLETELY ALL ALFRED MEANT
BY THIS, AND FROM THEN ON MISUNDERSTANDINGS BEGAN TO MELT AWAY."

REMEMBERED LAUGHTER: THE LIFE OF NOËL COWARD, BY COLE LESLEY

HATTIE'S THREE-EGG CAKE
(DELICIOUS)

2/3 cup butter (5 oz.)   2 tsp. baking powder
1½ cups sugar   2½ cups flour, sifted
3 eggs, beaten separately   1/2 tsp. vanilla
1 cup milk   1/2 tsp. almond extract

Cream butter and sugar. Beat egg yolks. Add to milk. Add baking powder to
flour and sift. Add yolks and milk mixture to sugar and butter; then alternate
adding flour and beaten whites. Lastly, add vanilla and almond extract. Pour
into deep tube pan—buttered—and bake in 360° oven 40–50 minutes. 1/2 cup
butter can be used, but [illegible in manuscript].

HATTIE SEDERHOLM WAS ALFRED'S MOTHER

"I WAS INSTRUCTED VERY EXPLICITLY THAT YOU SERVE THE MAIN COURSE
ONCE, THEN OFFER IT A SECOND TIME. YOU SERVE THE DESSERT ONCE AND
ONLY ONCE. YOU NEVER SERVED IT TWICE."

**R. PERKINS (NEPHEW OF TEN CHIMNEYS' CARETAKER B. PERKINS),
FROM TEN CHIMNEYS FOUNDATION'S ORAL HISTORIES PROJECT**

ALFRED'S DESSERT (ICE CREAM AND/OR ICE)

Make a ring or have a ring made of vanilla ice cream and raspberry ice. Coat the inside of ring mold with vanilla ice cream (about a scant 1/2 inch in thickness). Place in freezer for one hour to firm. Then fill with raspberry ice. Return to freezer for at least one hour. Turn out on a plate and fill center with halved strawberries that have been mixed and chilled with the grated rind of half an orange, 1/2 cup granulated sugar, 1/4 cup brandy and 1 teaspoon of Cointreau. This is good also with plain vanilla ice cream or plain raspberry ice.

ALFRED'S APPLE CAKE (SERVES 6)

1 1/2 cups cake flour, sifted before measuring	1 egg yolk
	3 Tbsp. milk
1/2 tsp. double-acting baking powder	1/2 cup melted butter, measured after melting
pinch of salt	

Filling:

4–5 apples	juice of 1/2 lemon

Glaze:

3/4 cup sugar	1/4 tsp. cinnamon
1 Tbsp. flour	3 Tbsp. melted butter

Sift into bowl cake flour, baking powder, and salt. Into this stir or mix with hands, egg yolk and milk, then stir in melted butter. It's a discouraging looking dough, curdled and greasy, but proceed to pour it into a shallow pan, 7" x 10" (is the best size), and push about with spoon or fingers until bottom of pan is covered evenly. Push half inch or so up sides to form a low "box." Set to one side while you peel, core, and slice lengthwise 4 or 5 apples, and mix them with the lemon juice. Arrange them on the dough in three even tightly fitting rows, the slices overlapping each other, and sprinkle over the glaze—sugar, flour, and cinnamon mixed and melted butter—and pat it on. Bake in 325° oven for 1 hour. Whipped cream may be served with it. Cherries or split and stoned plums may be substituted for apples but with not so great a success.

There is no use trying to get flavor out of a poor, tasteless apple. Pare and core firm ripe apples, leaving them whole. Squeeze into the core hole a rolled piece of apple peeling. Fit apples snugly into a casserole and pour on a little water, about a quarter way up. Sprinkle with sugar (white or brown or mixed), depending on taste. Dot with butter and bake in 400° oven until tops begin to brown. Then cover and bake until done but not mushy. Remove from oven; take out apple peeling and fill hole with jelly or jam. Sprinkle a little sugar (or apricot glaze) over entire surface and set under broiler for a few minutes.

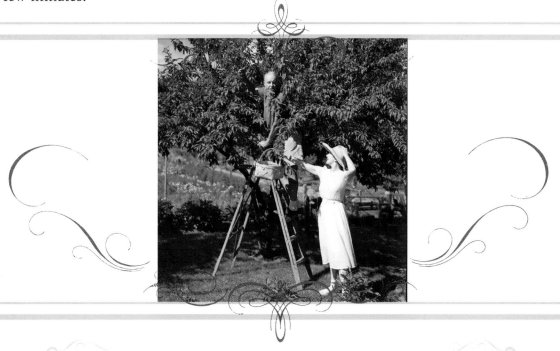

ALFRED'S BAVARIAN CREAM (SERVES 6–8)

1/2 cup sugar	1/2 tsp. vanilla or rum,
3 egg yolks	brandy, etc. to taste
1 cup milk, scalded	1 cup cream, whipped
1/8 tsp. salt	2 egg whites, beaten stiff,
	if desired

Beat sugar and egg yolks until light; add slowly the hot milk. Put in top of double boiler and cook, stirring constantly, until it thickens like a soft custard (when spoon is coated). Cool, add salt and flavoring, stirring occasionally. When it begins to thicken, fold in cream and, if desired, the egg whites. Pour into mold and chill for at least 3 hours. Unmold and serve with stewed fruit or fruit sauce.

ALFRED'S BLUEBERRY CAKE

1/2 cup butter (1/4 lb.)

1 cup sugar

2 eggs, well beaten

1 1/2 cups cake flour, measured after sifting

1 tsp. baking powder

1/2 tsp. salt

1/3 cup milk

1 1/2 cup blueberries

Cream butter and sugar; add beaten eggs and beat again. Sift flour with baking powder and salt, and stir in alternately with milk. Dredge blueberries plentifully with some flour and stir them carefully into the mixture. Pour into a buttered square pan. Sift white sugar generously over top (this forms a nice crust) and bake in a 340° oven (moderate) for 35 minutes. Serve hot, cut in squares, with butter.

ALFRED'S BROWN-EDGE BUTTER WAFERS

1/4 pound butter

1/2 cup sugar

1 egg

3/4 cup flour

1/2 tsp. vanilla

Cream butter and sugar. Add egg and mix. Add flour and vanilla and mix. This will be a soft dough. Drop onto ungreased cookie sheet using a teaspoon. Leave about 2 1/2 inches between cookies, as dough spreads. Bake at 350° for 10 minutes—or until edges brown. Remove from pan immediately and cool on waxed paper until crisp. Makes 40-50 cookies.

ALFRED'S BROWNIES (MAKES ABOUT 20)

1/2 cup butter (4 oz.)	1/2 tsp. baking powder,
1 cup sugar	any type
2 eggs, beaten	1/2 tsp. vanilla
2 squares chocolate, melted	1 cup chopped walnuts
1/2 cup cake flour, sifted before measuring	

Cream butter with sugar. Add 2 well-beaten eggs; stir. Add 2 squares melted chocolate; stir. Then stir in gradually flour sifted with baking powder, then vanilla, and finally the nuts. Mix well. Pour into a buttered shallow pan (7" x 10") and bake in 325° oven for 35 minutes. Cut into squares while warm, but cool before removing.

ALFRED'S CHEESECAKE (EASILY SERVES 8)

Crust:

2/3 package zwieback (4 oz.)	1/2 tsp. cinnamon
2/3 cup sugar	1/3 cup butter

With rolling pin, crush zwieback into fine crumbs. Add sugar, cinnamon, and melted butter. Set aside 1/2 cup of this to cover top of cake. Butter well an 8" springform pan and press mixture on side and bottom of form.

Filling:

1 cup sugar	1 cup cream
4 eggs	$1^1/_2$ pounds cottage cheese,
1/8 tsp. salt	without cream
juice and rind of 1/2 lemon	4 Tbsp. flour, level
1/4 tsp. vanilla	

Beat sugar and eggs together until light. Then stir in salt, lemon juice and grated peel, and vanilla; then add the cream, followed by the cheese, and then the flour. Beat well. Strain through a sieve and beat again. Pour into zwieback-lined form. Sprinkle the 1/2 cup crumbs you've set aside over top and bake in a 325° oven for at least 1 hour. Then turn off heat, open oven door a crack, and let cake remain in oven for another hour, or until cool. Remove springform ring (first running knife around inside), and place cake on plate. Do not try to remove from tin bottom.

133

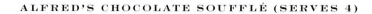

ALFRED'S CHOCOLATE SOUFFLÉ (SERVES 4)

3 Tbsp. flour	2 squares bitter chocolate,
2 Tbsp. butter	melted
2 cups milk, heated	1/2 cup sugar
4 eggs, separated	

Make same as Cheescake (see page 133) except, instead of cheese, add to the white sauce first the sugar and then the melted chocolate; cool. Then add the egg yolks. Pour this over the whipped egg whites, etc. When smooth and foaming, pour into a 7" casserole, set in a pan of hot water, and bake in a 350° oven for 50 to 60 minutes or a little longer. Remove and serve at once with:

Rum Sauce:

Soft Custard Recipe (see page	1 cup cream, whipped
144), or 1/2 a recipe	rum, to taste

Fold whipped cream into the soft custard; add rum to taste.

ALFRED'S COEUR À LA CRÈME (SERVES 4–5)

1¹/₂ pounds cottage cheese,	1/2 cup heavy cream,
small curd	whipped stiff
1 cream cheese, small	salt to taste
1/2 cup sour cream	

Combine cottage cheese, cream cheese, and sour cream and beat until smooth. Then fold in whipped cream until all is soft and velvety. Season to taste with salt. Line heart-shaped coeur à la crème baskets with cheesecloth wrung out in cold water and pour into these the above mixture—or, if no baskets available, substitute a low mold. Chill thoroughly 4–5 hours. Turn out on serving dish, remove cheesecloth, and serve with slightly sweetened strawberries—fresh or frozen.

ALFRED'S COEUR À LA CRÈME 2

1/4 pound cream cheese
1/2 pound cottage cheese
pinch of salt

1/2 cup sweet or sour cream
1 tsp. powdered sugar

Stir all together and put through a fine sieve. If too stiff, add a little cream or milk. Line small heart-shaped wicker baskets with damp cheesecloth. Fill with cheese and place in icebox to mold. When "set," remove from basket and cloth and serve with bar-le-duc or strawberry jam.

ALFRED'S COTTAGE CHEESE PIE (SERVES 6)

Crumb Shell:

Set oven at 350°. Press through fine sieve 1 pound dry cottage cheese.

1/3 cup sugar
1/2 tsp. salt
1 cup light cream
3 eggs, well beaten

2 Tbsp. butter, melted
grated rind and juice of
    1 lemon

Pour into crumb shell. Bake until firm (about 1 hour).

"THIS AFTERNOON, I AM GOING TO THE LUNTS TO
BE TAUGHT HOW TO MAKE PIES!"

NOËL COWARD FROM *THE NOËL COWARD DIARIES*

ALFRED'S CRÈME BRÛLÉE

4 egg yolks   1 pint heavy cream
2 Tbsp. sugar

Beat together egg yolks and sugar in bowl. Heat cream in double boiler. When very hot (not boiling), pour slowly over sugar and egg mixture. Return all to double boiler and cook, stirring constantly until it coats spoon. Sprinkle brown sugar (or maple sugar) [brown sugar not mentioned in ingredients] over top, 1/2" in thickness. Put under a hot flame until a crust is formed. (Do not leave in oven long.) Let cool; then return to icebox and leave until cold. Serve from baking dish, with strawberries or raspberries or alone.

"LUNT HAS EVEN DELVED INTO THE INTRICACIES OF BAKING
BREAD, CAKE, AND PUFF PASTRY."

"HE LIKES TO COOK," *BETTER HOMES & GARDENS,* AUGUST 1962

ALFRED'S CRANBERRY JELLY IN MOLD
(SERVES 6)

1 quart cranberries (1 lb.)   2 cups sugar
2 cups boiling water

Put cranberries into kettle, add 2 cups boiling water, cover, and boil 4 minutes. Strain through sieve. Return to kettle. Add 2 cups sugar and bring to boiling point. Remove from fire. Pour into mold (6 cups) and cool.

For cream puffs or "profiteroles," plain or shaped as swans, éclairs, or tiny savory ones for cocktails: 1 cup water, 1/2 cup butter, 1 cup flour, 3 eggs. Bring water to boil in saucepan; add butter and, when melted, add all the flour and cook, stirring until mixture slides off sides of pan. Cool slightly, and then beat in eggs one at a time. Dough slips around a bit, but persevere. Drop spoonful of this or squeeze through pastry tube (lumps a little bigger than a golf ball) onto well-greased baking sheet (use vegetable shortening or cooking oil), placing them at least 2 or 3 inches apart. Bake for 20 minutes in 450° oven. Reduce heat to 325° and bake 20 minutes longer, or until a light brown. Don't peek at them for at least 30 minutes. Remove from sheet and cool. Cut open and fill with whipped cream, or make smaller ones and fill with ice cream and pour over a rich chocolate sauce and whipped cream from pastry tube. For cocktails, squeeze dough from pastry tube into pieces not bigger than one inch. Fill when cold with any highly seasoned "spread" you fancy. For swans, make six ordinary-sized puffs as oblong in shape as possible and squeeze out separate thin $2\frac{1}{2}$" strips on pan in shape of long esses. Bake; when done and cool, cut an opening in top and fill with whipped cream, and stick on one end of each an "ess," which will represent the swan's neck. Set them on chocolate sauce. If expert, you can draw wings with a thick chocolate sauce through a fine-nozzled pastry tube.

ALFRED'S ECLAIRS

Squeeze cream puff mixture through a pastry tube in oblongs 4" long and 1" wide on buttered cookie sheets. They must be 2" apart. Bake as above and when cool, split on one side and fill with custard, chocolate, or whipped cream; frost with chocolate.

ALFRED'S EMPEROR CAKE (SERVES 25–30)
(A COLOSSAL SUCCULENT CONFECTION.)

A dazzling, eight-layered, taste-tempting triumph, recently smuggled from the Imperial archives of Austrian culinary art.

Cake:

12 eggs, separated	1½ cups cake flour, sifted
1 cup sugar	before measuring
6 Tbsp. water	2 tsp. baking powder
1 tsp. vanilla	

Beat egg yolks until light. Add sugar and continue beating for 15 minutes or until thick and pale yellow. Stir in water, vanilla, and flour, sifted with the baking powder. Fold in stiffly beaten whites. This is baked in four layers, so butter a shallow pan, 15½" x 11"; pour in 1/4 of the batter, which should barely cover bottom, and bake in a 350° oven for 15 minutes. Then bake three more layers. Use a spatula to remove, as cake is likely to stick. Set to one side on wax paper. One on top of another will do no harm.

Filling and Glaze:

3/4 pound sweet chocolate	1¼ cups strong coffee
2¼ cups powdered sugar,	1¼ pounds unsalted butter
divided	

Cook chocolate, 1⅛ cups sugar, and coffee slowly until it forms a soft ball in cold water. Cream butter with remaining sugar until light, and stir into chocolate mixture. Put aside 2/3 cup of this for glaze. Then divide the remainder in eight equal parts (use coffee cups) and place in refrigerator until firm enough to spread. Cut cake layers in half, spread with 1 cup "filling," place another layer over this, spread with a cup of filling, and repeat until all is used. Then carefully spread over top and sides the cup of "glaze" you set to one side. This cake keeps for weeks in a refrigerator.

ALFRED'S FLAKY PASTRY
(SURE-FIRE PIE CRUST!)

NOTE: THE INGREDIENT
"1/2 CUP BUTTER"
IS NOT MENTIONED
SPECIFICALLY IN
INSTRUCTIONS BELOW.

1/2 cup butter

1/2 cup vegetable
    shortening or lard

1³/₄ cups flour

6 Tbsp. ice water

All ingredients should be very cold, so it is not a bad idea to put the bowl of flour into the refrigerator for several hours or so, as well as the shortening cut into pieces the size of small [illegible in manuscript]. When all ingredients are cold, add the shortening to the flour and quickly chop it in with a pastry mixer (or with two knives) until the pieces of fat are no longer—or smaller—than plump peas. Don't mash it down too heavily—chop away and keep it light, lifting it up from the bottom now and then. (If the shortening is chopped too fine, the pastry will not be so flaky.) Add the 6 tablespoons of ice water one at a time, and form the dough into a ball; wrap in wax paper or aluminum foil and cool in the icebox for 3 hours—or overnight. This dough will keep for a week.

ALFRED'S FUDGE CAKE

2 cups sugar

1 cup cooking oil

2 eggs

3 cups all-purpose flour

3/4 cup unsweetened cocoa

2 tsp. baking powder

2 tsp. soda

1¹/₂ tsp. salt

1 cup hot coffee

1 cup buttermilk

1 tsp. vanilla

Generously butter and lightly flour 10" tube or Bundt pan. In large bowl combine sugar, oil, and eggs; beat 1 minute. Add remaining ingredients; beat 3 minutes. Bake at 350° for approximately 70–75 minutes.

Glaze:

1 cup powdered sugar

3 Tbsp. cocoa

2 Tbsp. butter

2 tsp. vanilla

1–3 Tbsp. hot water

ALFRED'S HAZELNUT COOKIES, FILLED

1/2 cup butter	pinch of salt
1/4 cup sugar	1/2 tsp. vanilla
1 1/2 cups sifted flour, measure after sifting	1 glass currant jelly uncooked icing recipe
1/2 cup grated hazelnuts	(see page 156)

Cream butter and sugar. Thoroughly stir in flour, then the nuts, salt, and vanilla. Form into a roll 2" in diameter. Wrap in wax paper and put in icebox overnight. The next day, slice off very thin cookies and place them on ungreased baking sheet. Bake in a slow oven, 275°, for 30 minutes or until edges turn a light brown. While still warm, spread a thin layer of currant jelly (beaten) on half a cookie and cover it with another; ice. Ground almonds may be used instead of hazelnuts. And cookies are good plain without jelly or icing. Makes about 30 to 40 cookies.

ALFRED'S HONEY, CARAMEL, & SOFT CUSTARDS

Honey Custard:

3 cups milk	1/2 cup strained honey
3 eggs	2 Tbsp. sugar

Proceed as in Baked Custard (see page 126).

Caramel Custard:

1 cup sugar	3 Tbsp. boiling water

Same as above, except coat bottom and sides of baking dish with the above ingredients. Melt sugar in frying pan until golden in color; add hot water and stir constantly until a syrup is formed. Pour this into baking dish and move it around and about until the bottom and all sides are covered. When cool, pour in custard and bake in pan of hot water in 325° oven for 1 hour or until an inserted knife comes out clean. Cool. Unmold onto a shallow bowl. Decorate top with split whole blanched almonds or sprinkle over it crushed almond brittle.

Quick Soft Custard (Cold):

1 pint vanilla ice cream	1 or more tsp. Jamaica rum

Use an ice cream that is not too potent with vanilla. Soften ice cream and beat in the rum. Serve very cold.

144

ALFRED'S JUNKET

Milk   jelly, any kind
Junket tablets

Make junket according to directions on package. Before serving, place a
generous spoonful of jelly in center of individual dish. Serve Alfred's Spritz
Cookies or Esses (see page 152) or nut cookies with this.

"WELL, MISS FONTANNE, SHE LOVED LEMON PIE. SHE LOVED
LEMON PIE. IT WAS ONE OF HER FAVORITE DESSERTS."

M. ROLAND (WORKED FOR THE LUNTS)
FROM TEN CHIMNEYS FOUNDATION'S ORAL HISTORIES PROJECT

ALFRED'S LEMON PIE

1 cup sugar   2 egg yolks
1/4 cup flour   1 whole egg
1 lemon, grated rind   1 Tbsp. butter
    and juice   1 cup hot water

Put all ingredients in double boiler. Cook, stirring constantly until thick. Pour
into baked pie shell and top with meringue.

Meringue:

Beat 2 egg whites stiff; add 4 tablespoons sugar, one at a time. Continue beating.
Add 2 tablespoons sugar and stir one minute. Bake in 350° oven until lightly
browned.

ALFRED'S MAZARINS (MAKES 15–16 IN SMALL TINS)

Cake:

1/2 cup butter	1¼ cups flour, measured
1/4 cup sugar	after sifting
1 egg yolk	

Filling:

1/2 cup sugar	2 eggs
3/4 cup ground, blanched	2 Tbsp. grated pistachio
almonds	nuts

Cream butter and sugar, beat in egg yolk, and then gradually add the flour. Make into a long roll and cut off pieces or just take lumps from dough and press with fingers into small greased pan to the thickness of 1/4". Beat the sugar, almonds, and eggs together until fluffy. Fill lined pans with this 3/4 full. Set pans on baking sheet and bake in 350° oven for 10 to 15 minutes. Never mind if the filling "drops". Remove from pans at once. Set them on rack and frost tops with 1 cup powdered sugar mixed with 2 tablespoons water. Sprinkle with grated pistachio nuts. These are truly delicious when served fresh with afternoon coffee. Diamond or oval shaped tins 4" long and 1/2" deep are best. If baked in larger round tins, with two strips of dough crossed over top they are called polyneès.

MRS. SEDERHOLM'S DOUGHNUTS (MAKES 36 DOUGHNUTS)

1¾ cups sugar	1 tsp. soda added
pinch of salt	1/2 cup buttermilk
3 eggs, well beaten, and add	2 cups flour, measured after
2 Tbsp. melted butter	sifting, sifted with
1/2 cup sour cream with	1 tsp. baking powder

[No instructions on preparation in manuscript]

HATTIE SEDERHOLM WAS ALFRED'S MOTHER

4 oranges, peeled and sliced very thin

Thinly peel 1 or 2 tablespoons of the outer skin cut into very fine strips. Place these strips into 2 cups cold water. Bring to a boil and let simmer for a few minutes and then drain. Make a syrup of the juice of 1 orange, 2 cups of water, and 1/2 cup sugar (or as much sugar as desired). Sprinkle slices of orange with the shredded peelings. Pour over the hot syrup and let cool. Keeps for days.

"ALFRED LIKED ORANGES, SLICED VERY THIN, AND

SPRINKLED WITH SUGAR FOR BREAKFAST."

WISCONSIN STATE HISTORICAL SOCIETY,

"HOME LIFE WITH THE LUNTS" BY CAROLYN EVERY, 1983

ALFRED'S PASTRY FOR PIROG (PIEROGI)

1 1/2 cup flour, measure after sifting	1/2 cup butter
1/2 tsp. salt	1/2 cup ice water, approximately

Sift flour and salt. Work in butter until it resembles coarse meal. Mix in the water, maybe a little less than indicated. The dough should be slightly stiff. Roll out 1/4" thick and proceed with filling. Brush with egg yolk mixed with a little water. Bake in 375° oven for 3/4 to 1 hour.

Poach pears or pear halves in port wine. Cool. Sprinkle with finely ground, darkly browned almonds. Decorate with whipped cream.

ALFRED'S PECAN COOKIES (MAKES 24)

1/4 pound butter	1 cup flour, measured after
3/4 cup powdered sugar,	sifting
divided	2 ounces chopped pecans

Cream butter and 1/4 cup sugar. Add flour gradually and then chopped pecans. Mix well. Shape (with hands) into small balls or fat crescents. Place on buttered cookie sheet and bake in 275° oven about 30 minutes. Roll in 1/2 cup powdered sugar while still warm. When placing cookie balls on sheet, press down with thumb making a slight dent in center. They should not be more than 2" in diameter.

ALFRED'S RÖTGRÖT AND RASPBERRY SYRUP (SERVES 4)

Rötgröt:

4 cups red raspberry syrup	ground almonds
3 Tbsp. cornstarch or potato flour	cream

Bring the fruit syrup to a boil. Stir in the cornstarch mixed in 1/3 cup water. Bring to a boil again, stirring constantly. Pour into a flat glass serving bowl and let cool but do not put in refrigerator. It should be the consistency of a thick sauce—not firm. Serve with ground blanched almonds and cream.

Raspberry Syrup:

2–3 quarts raspberries	sugar

Put raspberries in kettle. Add 1 cup of water, cover, and heat through. Strain through a thin cloth. To each cup of juice add 3/4 cup sugar. Put in kettle; boil 1 minute. Remove all scum and bottle hot. Canned red raspberries, strained, can be used. If a more tart flavor is desired, add a few tablespoons of currant jelly or juice. If syrup seems too sweet or the flavor too strong, dilute with water.

1 yeast cake (1 oz.)

1/2 cup milk

pinch of salt

2 egg yolks

1 cup sour cream

1/4 pound butter

1/4 pound oleomargarine

3$^{1}/_{2}$ to 4 cups flour

white sugar, cinnamon, brown
sugar, raisins and/or
chopped walnuts

Dissolve yeast in sugar (crumble yeast in cup, add sugar, stir, and the yeast will dissolve); stir into lukewarm milk and then add salt and the 2 egg yolks and sour cream. Stir in flour gradually and mix well. Begin with 3$^{1}/_{2}$ cups flour, but if still too sticky to work, add a little more at a time, but the dough should be soft. If dough is too thin to handle, add a little flour but the less the better. Roll out dough in a rectangular piece 24" x 14" on a floured board. Dot with half the softened shortening. Fold in three as you would a napkin, the end toward you to the center, the farthest edge from you over that and toward you. Turn at right angles and roll into another rectangular piece and dot with remaining shortening. Fold again and roll. Repeat this three times. If some of the fat oozes through, sprinkle with a little flour and proceed as if it didn't matter, which it doesn't. Keep board as well as rolling pin dusted with flour. The dough is so rich you can't hurt it. When you've finished the rolling, wrap it in a clean cloth or wax paper and keep in the icebox overnight. The next day, roll it out into a piece 24" x 20"; sprinkle with white sugar, cinnamon, brown sugar, and chopped nuts. Roll up like jelly roll, and cut into 1/2" or 1" pieces. Set in buttered muffin pans or in a frying pan in which you have melted 3 tablespoons butter. Let cool and add brown sugar and crushed pecans (on this place the rolls). Let rise about 1 to 1$^{1}/_{2}$ hours, and bake in a 350° oven. They burn quickly, so watch carefully. Bake 25 minutes or until brown.

"WE DID NOT HAVE DESSERT OFTEN, EXCEPT FOR SOME ELEGANT ICE CREAM, A FAVORITE. AND A CLABBERED SWEDISH CREAM CHEESE OF WHICH THEY [THE LUNTS] WERE FOND."

WISCONSIN STATE HISTORICAL SOCIETY,

"HOME LIFE WITH THE LUNTS" BY CAROLYN EVERY, 1983

ALFRED'S SPRITZ COOKIES OR ESSES
(MAKES ABOUT 50 ESSES)

1/2 cup butter (4 oz.)

3/4 cup sugar (or 1 cup)

1 egg

1¹⁄₂ cups flour, measured
    after sifting

1 Tbsp. ground almonds

1/2 tsp. almond extract and
    vanilla mixed

5 ground, bitter almonds

Cream butter and sugar. Add beaten egg and then dry ingredients and extracts. When too difficult to mix with spoon, use hands. Put dough in pastry tube, using "star" cutter, and press out esses about 2" long on greased cookie sheet. Bake 10 minutes in 400° oven until golden in color.

ALFRED'S SUNDAY CAKE (SERVES 6–8)

NOTE: THE INGREDIENT "BAKING POWDER" IS NOT MENTIONED IN INSTRUCTIONS BELOW.

2/3 cup sugar

2 eggs

2/3 cup butter

1/2 tsp. baking powder
    (cream of tartar type)

1/4 tsp. vanilla

3/4 cup cake flour,
    measured after
    sifting

butter and crumbs for pan

This cake never fails. (It may be imagination, but the texture of this cake always seems best when made on a hot day or in an overheated kitchen, and hand-beaten with a rotary beater and wooden spoon.) It's much like an old-fashioned English Madeira cake and quite as delicious. (It is good without frosting; you can dust with powdered sugar.) Beat sugar and eggs together until light; add to creamed butter. (It must be mixed in this way.) Beat in sugar, then vanilla, and then the flour gradually. Don't try this in electric mixer. Butter and crumb lightly an 8" iron frying pan (8" at top) or a cake pan of same size. That is, butter inside of pan and sprinkle with very fine bread or cracker crumbs. Turn pan around and dump out excess crumbs. (Flour can be used.) Pour in dough and bake in 325° oven 1 hour. Turn out at once.

NOTE: A VERSION OF THIS RECIPE RAN IN THE NOVEMBER 1956 ISSUE OF *WOMAN'S HOME COMPANION*.

Caramel (to coat ring):

1 cup sugar   3 Tbsp. boiling water

Pudding:

NOTE: THE INGREDIENT "2 TBSP. SUGAR" IS NOT MENTIONED IN INSTRUCTIONS BELOW.

1/2 cup butter   8 Tbsp. Swedish punch
2/3 cup flour   or rum
1 1/2 cups milk, heated   1 cup cream, whipped
2 Tbsp. sugar   punch or rum
4 eggs, separated

Melt cup of sugar in frying pan and when gold in color, add hot water and stir until syrupy. Pour into ring mold and move it about until all sides are coated. Melt butter; stir in flour, mixing thoroughly. Add hot milk; stir until thick. Let cool and add egg yolks, one at a time. Add punch or rum. Lastly, fold in stiffly beaten egg whites. Pour into ring mold, tie a piece of waxed paper over top, and bake in a pan of hot water in a 350° oven for 50 to 60 minutes. Let stand 3 to 5 minutes before unmolding. Serve hot or cold with whipped cream flavored with punch or rum.

ALFRED'S THREE-EGG CAKE

1/2 cup butter   2 tsp. double-acting baking
1 1/2 cups sugar   powder
3 eggs, separated   1/2 tsp. vanilla extract
2 1/2 cups cake flour,   1/2 tsp. almond extract
    measured after sifting

NOTE: EXTRACTS ARE NOT MENTIONED IN INSTRUCTIONS BELOW.

Cream butter and sugar; stir in slightly beaten egg yolks. Then sift in flour and baking powder mixed. Lastly, fold in egg whites. Pour into buttered pan with funnel (tube pan, 9 1/2" at top and 4" deep) and bake 55 minutes in 325° oven. Remove from pan when cake has cooled but is still warm.

ALFRED'S UNCOOKED ICING

1 cup powdered sugar
2 Tbsp. hot water

Flavoring, vanilla or almond

ALFRED'S TIPSY PARSON

stale or fresh sponge cake
strawberry jam
Madeira and brandy

Alfred's Soft Custard recipe
(see page 144)
macaroons
split blanched almonds

Use stale or fresh homemade, or the baker's best quality, sponge cake. Cut slices 2" to 3" wide, spread with strawberry jam, and fill the bottom of a glass flat-bottomed bowl with them, one layer only. Drip over each piece a tablespoon of Madeira and 1 teaspoon brandy, or more if you wish it really "speeded up." Let stand until sponge cake absorbs all of the liquor. Before serving barely cover with a soft custard, and on top of that a layer of whipped cream. Decorate with halved macaroons and split blanched almonds.

"HE [ALFRED LUNT] IS THE ARTIST WHOSE GENIUS HAS GONE
INTO THE SOUFFLÉ YOU EAT. HE IS THE SOUL OF TORMENT,
HANGING ON YOUR OPINION OF A SAUCE."

COLLIER'S, "THE CHEF'S ROLE," 1933

ALFRED'S BEST RUM CAKE EVER

1 or 2 quarts rum	1 tsp. baking powder
1 cup butter	1 tsp. soda
1 tsp. sugar	1/2 pint lemon juice
2 large eggs	1 cup brown sugar
1 cup dried fruit	1 cup nuts

Before you start, sample the rum for quality. Good, isn't it? Now go ahead. Select a large mixing bowl, measuring cup, etc. Check the rum again. It must be just right. To be sure rum is of the highest quality, pour one level cup of rum into a glass and drink it as fast as you can. Repeat. With an electric mixer, beat 1 cup of butter in a large fluffy bowl. Add 1 seaspoon of thugar and beat again. Meanwhile, make sure that the rum is of the highest quality. Try another cup. Open second quart if necessary. Add 2 arge leggs, 2 cups fried druit, and beat till high. If druit gets stuck in beaters, just pry it loose with a drewscriver. Sample the rum again, checking for tonsisticity. Next, sift 3 cups of pepper or salt (it really doesn't matter). Sample the rum again. Sift 1/2 pint of lemon juice. Fold in chopped butter and strained nuts. Add 1 babblespoon of brown thugar, or whatever color you can find. Wix mel. Crease oven and turn cake pan to 350 gradees. Now pour the whole mess into the coven and ake. Check the rum again, and bo to ged.

Merry Christmas

LYNN FONTANNE
ALFRED LUNT

SAUCES

ALFRED, SHOWN HERE IN HIS 80S, CONTINUED HIS
CULINARY PURSUITS WELL INTO HIS RETIREMENT TO
TEN CHIMNEYS.

ALFRED LUNT'S
COOKBOOK
TESTER'S EDITION

PHOTO BY WARREN O'BRIEN FROM
THE O'BRIEN FAMILY COLLECTION AT
WHS © TCF

ALFRED'S CUMBERLAND SAUCE (SERVES 4–6)
(FOR HOT HAM OR SMOKED TONGUE)

1 tsp. onions, finely chopped	1 tsp. bottled horseradish
1 Tbsp. orange peel, cut into very fine strips, 1–2" long	juice of 1 orange
	juice of 1/2 lemon
1 Tbsp. lemon peel, cut into very fine strips, 1–2" long	1/2 tsp. English mustard
	dash cayenne pepper
1/2 glass currant jelly	1/3 cup port wine

Put the onions in a little water, bring to boil, boil for 2 minutes, and strain through a sieve. Do the same with the orange and lemon peels, although they may be boiled together. Melt the currant jelly and stir in all the other ingredients. Let stand awhile in double boiler before serving. Thin pieces of orange and lemon peel can easily be shaved off with a vegetable peeler and then cut into fine strips with a very sharp knife.

ALFRED'S HOLLANDAISE SAUCE (SERVES 4)

1/2 cup butter	cayenne pepper
$1^1/_2$ tsp. lemon juice, or more, to taste	pinch of salt, more later, if desired
2 egg yolks	

This is not apt to curdle if made in an enamel double boiler and the water beneath never allowed to quite boil, just steam. If it does boil, lift upper pot immediately and lower heat. In fact, never let go of the handle and be on the safe side. Use wooden spoon not too big either. Cut butter in 1" pieces and set on plate at side easily reached. Mix lemon juice, egg yolks, cayenne pepper and pinch of salt in upper pot of double boiler. Then place over steaming water in lower part. Stir constantly. Add a piece of butter and when melted, add another. Repeat this until all butter is used. If, in the process, the mixture either looks as if it would curdle or does curdle, quickly add a tablespoon of boiling water (from below). Add one anyway at the end and more salt and lemon juice if you care to. Pour into bowl and serve with asparagus, broccoli, boiled fish, etc. Never make more than you'll need as it's expensive and of little use when cold.

ALFRED'S HORSERADISH SAUCE (SERVES 4-6)
(WITH WHIPPED CREAM)

bottled horseradish
1/2 cup whipped cream

salt, to taste
sugar, to taste

Be sure horseradish is not brown. Press out liquid by pressing it through a sieve. Beat it into whipped cream, adding salt and sugar to taste (not much sugar). Serve in separate bowl.

ALFRED'S LOBSTER SAUCE

Alfred's White or Cream Sauce,
    Light (see page 164)
1/4 cup sherry

1/4 cup cream
1/2 pound fresh lobster meat

Add sherry and cream to sauce, then lobster. Let stand 15 minutes and serve. Or use Alfred's light sauce. Mix 2 egg yolks with cream; stir into sauce carefully. Then add sherry and lobster.

ALFRED'S MINT SAUCE

1/4 cup water
1/4 cup vinegar

1/2 cup sugar
2 sprigs mint

Boil up and take out sprigs. Pour over 1/4 cup or more of mint leaves chopped. Let stand 15 to 20 minutes. Serve hot or cold.

ALFRED'S PAN GRAVY

Remove roast; skim off fat in pan. Sprinkle 2 tablespoons flour over juices, scraping sides and bottom, and mixing well. Add water to make 3 cups of gravy. If too thick, add more water. Salt and pepper to taste; strain and serve in separate bowl. If too light in color, add 1/2 to 1 teaspoon Kitchen Bouquet.

ALFRED'S QUICK CHOCOLATE SAUCE (SERVES 8)

1 cup best grade cocoa	1$\frac{1}{2}$ tsp. vanilla
1$\frac{1}{2}$ cups sugar	1/4 tsp. almond extract
1 cup boiling water	

NOTE: THE INGREDIENT "ALMOND EXTRACT" IS NOT MENTIONED IN INSTRUCTIONS BELOW.

Mix dry ingredients. Make a paste by adding 1/4 to 1/2 cup cold water. Beat smooth. Add cup of boiling water and cook 1 minute. Cool. Add vanilla. Cream or butter may be added to make a richer sauce.

ALFRED'S RUM SAUCE

Soft Custard recipe (see page 144), or 1/2 recipe	1 cup cream, whipped rum, to taste

Fold whipped cream into the soft custard; add rum to taste.

ALFRED'S SAUCE BÉARNAISE (SERVES 4)

This is made precisely like hollandaise (see page 160), only substitute 1 or 2 teaspoons tarragon vinegar for lemon juice, and at the finish, stir in one teaspoon chopped tarragon leaves, one teaspoon parsley, one teaspoon chives, and 1/2 teaspoon very finely chopped leek or onion. Just before serving, drop in a pinch of brown sugar. If this doesn't melt, stir it in. It is better to cook down (reduce) a scant 1/4 cup tarragon vinegar with 1/4 teaspoon chopped onions to 2 teaspoons (and strain), though if you haven't time, never mind.

"AT TEN CHIMNEYS HE RAISED HIS OWN FRUITS AND VEGETABLES, HIS OWN CHICKENS AND EGGS, MADE HIS OWN BUTTER MILKED FROM HIS OWN COWS. HE CANNED, MADE JAMS AND JELLIES, CREATED SPECIAL SAUCES."

FROM "LANDMARK" BY THE WAUKESHA COUNTY HISTORICAL SOCIETY, 1981

CLAGGETT WILSON PAINTING THE DRAWING ROOM CEILING AT TEN CHIMNEYS.

Light for Vegetables and Fish:

2 Tbsp. butter	1/4 tsp. salt
2 Tbsp. flour	1/8 tsp. white pepper
1 cup hot milk	

Heavy for Soufflés:

3 Tbsp. butter	1/4 tsp. salt
3 Tbsp. flour	1/8 tsp. white pepper
1 cup hot milk	

Stir butter and flour together in top of double boiler over boiling water; when butter is melted and blended, add the hot milk, stirring constantly. Stir until smooth. Then add the salt and pepper.

ALFRED LUNT CONDUCTING HIS CELEBRATED COOKING
CLASSES AT THE STAGE DOOR CANTEEN DURING WWII.
ALFRED DONATED ALL PROCEEDS TO THE WAR EFFORT.

ALFRED LUNT'S
COOKBOOK
TESTER'S EDITION

ALFRED'S QUICK RASPBERRY OR STRAWBERRY JAM
(GOOD FOR APARTMENT DWELLERS OR SMALL FAMILIES)

4 cups berries   4 cups sugar, divided

Put berries in kettle. Add 2 cups sugar and boil 3 minutes. Then add remaining 2 cups sugar and boil 2 minutes. Pour into bowl and leave overnight, stirring jam every time you feel like it. Bottle cold.

ALFRED'S BORDEAUX PICKLES

4 quarts sliced green tomatoes   12 large onions
4 quarts sliced cabbage   1 finely chopped green pepper

Mix all of these. Add 1/2 cup salt. Mix and let stand 1 hour. Then drain very dry.

1 quart cider vinegar   1 Tbsp. whole cloves
4 cups sugar   1 ounce mustard seed

Boil together one minute. Then add first ingredients and cook until cabbage is done. Bottle.

ALFRED'S SLICED CUCUMBER PICKLES (SWEET)
(REFRIGERATE)

7 cups thinly sliced cucumbers	1 cup thinly sliced green peppers
1 cup thinly sliced onions	

Put in bowl with 1 tablespoon salt. Leave 1½ hours or more. Stir and drain.

1 cup vinegar	1 tsp. celery seed
2 cups sugar	1 tsp. mustard seed

Boil five minutes. Cool and pour over pickles in jars. Push down. Cap and refrigerate.

ALFRED'S SWEET RED PEPPER JAM

9 large sweet red peppers	1½ cups vinegar
1/4 cup salt	2½ cups sugar

Chop or cut peppers into small pieces. Add water to cover. Stir in salt. Let stand 2 hours or more. Bring vinegar and sugar to a boil. Drain peppers; add to vinegar mixture. Boil slowly till syrupy (about 45–60 minutes). Pour into sterilized jars.

ALFRED'S SENFGURKEN

2 large, ripe (yellow)
cucumbers

Brine:
1/4 cup salt
3 cups water

Peel cucumbers and cut in quarters. Remove seeds and then cut into eighths—
6" to 7" long. Soak in brine for 12 hours. Drain cucumbers, place in sterilized
jars with a piece of fresh horseradish (peeled and cut in one-inch pieces)
[horseradish not mentioned in ingredients] and a teaspoonful of mustard seed
[mustard seed not mentioned in ingredients]. Over this, pour a hot solution of
1 cup white vinegar [vinegar not mentioned in ingredients] and 3 cups of water
(brought to a boil). Seal. Use after three months.

BEVERAGES

LYNN AND ALFRED ENJOYING A DRINK BY TEN CHIMNEYS'
CHARMING POOLHOUSE.

ALFRED'S COFFEE

With so many methods and contrivances to make coffee, it seems ridiculous to add an old-fashioned one. However, it's always satisfactory in the country kitchen and out of doors. Use an old-fashioned enamel pot with a snub nose spout at the top and 1 heaping tablespoon of ground coffee for each cup and one for the pot. Mix coffee, egg (shell and all), and enough cold water to make a paste in pot. Add boiling water (one cup to each spoon of coffee). Let come to a full boil; remove from flame and stir down. Repeat this twice more for three times in all. Then let boil steadily for 3 full minutes. Pull to one side. Add 1/2 cup cold water and let stand 3 minutes before using. Never let pot become cold and never try to reheat it.

ALFRED SERVING WORKERS.

ALFRED'S TEA

Englishmen tell you an earthenware teapot is best, maybe. Have the water hot and bubbling; pour some in the pot until it's heated, then pour water out. Put in a teaspoon of tea for each person and pour on boiling water, a cup to a spoon of tea, and be sure to bring the pot to the teakettle, not the teakettle to the pot. Fill an extra jug with hot water and use as desired.

INDEX

172

THE TOUR OF A *Lifetime*™

Ten Chimneys is a landmark unique among our national treasures. The estate's diverse collections and enchanting décor are comprised of the original pieces hand-picked by the Lunts in the 1920s, '30s, and '40s. And the magic is undiminished. Ten Chimneys has become a popular attraction for a wide variety of individuals wishing to experience the inspiration of this intimate historic site.

A HOME FOR THE *Arts*™

A true renaissance at Ten Chimneys is about more than restoring a historic house and opening its doors to the public. A diverse menu of programs, developed in collaboration with an impressive list of national advisors, will ensure that future generations will benefit from Ten Chimneys' rich history. Ten Chimneys Foundation supports exciting public programs (estate tours, exhibitions, readings, lectures, publications) as well as important specialized programs for theatre, arts, and arts education professionals (artistic retreats, theatre conferences, support for new endeavors, productions, and national programs).

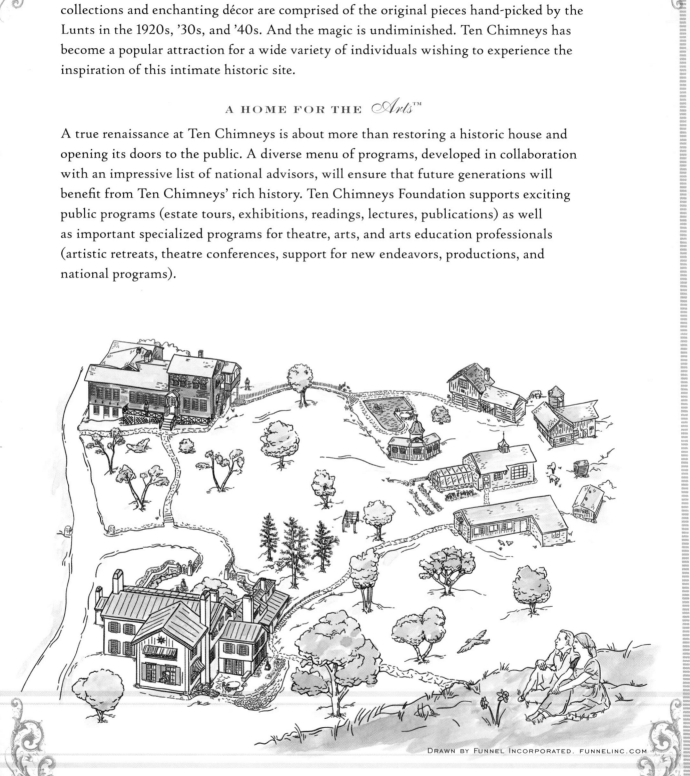

Drawn by Funnel Incorporated. funnelinc.com